CROSS-CULTURAL
COUNSELING

[handwritten notes, left column:]

Direct behaviour
≐ Client
centered

ender instruction

[handwritten notes, right column:]

A · Σ ⊢

— Submission as
positive value

— Schema to
family / father

— Schema to
community

CREATIVE PASTORAL CARE AND COUNSELING SERIES
Howard W. Stone and Howard Clinebell, coeditors

BOOKS IN THE SERIES

Counseling Adolescent Girls
Patricia H. Davis

Counseling Men
Philip L. Culbertson

Crisis Counseling (Revised Edition)
Howard W. Stone

Integrative Family Therapy
David C. Olsen

Risk Management
Aaron Liberman and Michael J. Woodruff

Woman-Battering
Carol J. Adams

CREATIVE PASTORAL CARE AND COUNSELING

CROSS-CULTURAL COUNSELING

AART M. VAN BEEK

FORTRESS PRESS   MINNEAPOLIS

To my son Andrew Ryan

Library of Congress Cataloging-in-Publication Data

van Beek, Aart.
    Cross-cultural counseling / Aart M. van Beek.
       p.   cm. — (Creative pastoral care and counseling series)
    Includes bibliographical references (p.).
    ISBN 0-8006-2666-4 (alk. paper)
    1. Pastoral counseling. 2. Cross-cultural counseling. I. Title.
  II. Series.
    BV4012.2.V25   1996
253.5—dc20   96.3214
                                                        CIP

The paper used in this publication meets the minimum requirements of American National Standard for Information Sciences—Permanence of Paper for Printed Library Materials, ANSI Z329.48-1984. ∞™

Manufactured in the U.S.A.   AF 1-2666

00   99   98   97   96   1   2   3   4   5   6   7   8   9   10

CONTENTS

FOREWORD

A variety of challenging changes are occurring in the pastoral care field in our day. Among these, intercultural conflicts are proliferating in our increasingly pluralistic, multicultural society and world. Clergy in many settings are confronting unprecedented opportunities to be agents of reconciliation and healing in their ministry with people from ethnic, language, class, and religious backgrounds radically different from their own. As a new century dawns, the need for the understanding and skills necessary to respond to these challenges undoubtedly will increase, even in formerly homogeneous cultural communities.

All this makes Aart van Beek's book a valuable contribution to the sparse resources in this area of pastoral care and counseling. In its brief scope, this volume highlights major insights and methods that are required in the difficult ministry of creating therapeutic communication bridges that connect people across cultural chasms.

The author brings to this book his own rich multicultural experiences, both personal and professional. He was born in the Netherlands and received his early education there. I first knew him while he was studying for a professional doctorate in pastoral psychology and counseling at the School of Theology in Claremont, California. Subsequently, the author was active in multicultural caring in various contexts, including counseling with Native Americans, Asian Americans, Latin Americans, and African Americans. In addition, he has rich personal experience in his marriage and family relations with the Chinese American/Vietnamese American culture.

Later Aart van Beek served for several years in Indonesia developing clinical training programs, doing supervision, and teaching with the Indonesian Christian Association of Health Services. His deep understanding of the Indonesian language and culture is reflected in the books he wrote on pastoral counseling in Indonesian, and his interpretation of lectures on pastoral care (including several by this editor). He also researched, wrote, and had published a history of the rulers and the ancient royal palaces in Yogyakarta and Solo, the historic cities in central Java, Indonesia.

While in Indonesia, van Beek completed a Ph.D. with the faculty of the Southeast Asia Graduate School of Theology. His dissertation research focused on cross-cultural counseling from theological and psychosocial perspectives. It is fortunate for our field that he has drawn on his significant research findings to write this practice-oriented book for clergy and other counselors.

This book, within its brief scope, sheds valuable light on doing multicultural caring and counseling in North America. Many of its insights are also relevant to cross-cultural counseling in other countries. The author focuses on the essential skills required for this caring ministry, making these concrete by case illustrations from a variety of cultures with which he has firsthand experience. He shows how differences in cultural codes and worldviews, between caregivers and care-receivers, pose crucial issues in the helping process. After exploring the importance of developing a communication bridge between these divergent orientations, he explores the use of biblical stories as vehicles of caring contact. In addition, van Beek reflects helpfully on cross-cultural pastoral assessment and family pastoral care, and then gives pointers for working pastorally with Americans of African, Latino, Asian, and Native backgrounds.

Those of us who developed the guidelines for this series expect that each book will provide practical insights and skills for caring and counseling work with persons struggling with a particular problem encountered regularly by those in ordained but also lay ministry. As I believe you will soon discover, this expectation is fulfilled by this volume. Beyond the resources available in these pages for helping others across cultures, you may also gain enhanced understanding of your own cultural identity—an invaluable asset for helping others!

HOWARD CLINEBELL

ACKNOWLEDGMENTS

I would like to express my gratitude to the editorial team of the Creative Pastoral Care and Counseling Series for their support and thoughtful criticism. I wish to thank especially Howard Clinebell, earlier my advisor for both a professional project and a dissertation, whose insight has been instrumental to my professional development.

Furthermore I am grateful to my wife Carolyn, whose own cultural experience makes my life a continuous cross-cultural journey and who keeps me humbly aware of my shortcomings as a cross-cultural caregiver.

I am indebted to the persons who have granted me the privilege of seeing the world from the vantage point of their experience: the Latino American students in Texas, the Korean American church youth, the Chinese and Vietnamese half of our family, and the African American clients in California, the patients at Hawaii State Hospital, the Shoshone and Paiute of the Inter-Mountain West, as well as the otherwise American. Last but not least, I wish to recognize the Indonesians whose many worlds within a giant nation-archipelago deepened my awareness of the unique challenges in the field of cross-cultural pastoral care and counseling.

As I finish this small contribution, I am reminded of the many worlds my sons Drew (to whom I dedicate this book) and Daniel have been born into as cross-cultural world-citizens. My hope is that one day, in a more harmonious world, they will glance at this book's cover and wonder why their father felt he needed to write it in the first place.

INTRODUCTION
A CONTEMPORARY IMPERATIVE

The increased interest in cross-cultural issues, however fashionable it may seem, is certainly not coincidental. On a global scale we have been witnessing a surge in expressions of cultural identity. In North America this has been a predominantly peaceful and positive development spurred by a heightened awareness of identity other than "American" or "Canadian." African American experience encouraged other Americans to discover their historical roots in the early 1980s. A new wave of immigrants from Asia with strong cultural cohesion reminded Americans of their own cultural particularity. A significant number of the quality novelists writing in the English language are "hyphenated" Americans with Indian, Chinese, African, and Cuban roots. In their work they emphasize the uniqueness of their own and their families' cultural experience. They thereby underscore the notion that the concept of the "melting pot" that merged the original cultures of new Americans is no longer valid. The idea of "tossed salad" has been proposed in recent years, for in that healthy nutritional mix, each element retains its identity in the North American bowl. Yet the Los Angeles riots of the spring of 1992 perhaps rebuff that notion. The idea of a multicultural "potluck" comes to mind: each city or region creates its own cultural display, while leaving open the option of exploring a new experience. But this image may be no more appropriate.

While cultural identity as of late has been strengthened in its particularity (Latino, African American, Jewish, Anglo Saxon, and so forth), the different cultural groups have much in common: the worldview of

11

freedom and economic opportunity, the longing for security, and the sense of belonging on a common soil.

Cross-cultural issues are pushed to the surface in the tension between otherness and commonality. This tension can be creative or, among other things, lead to destructive eruptions of violence. Because of the dangerous intercultural conflicts recurring in our day and age, an awareness of these issues becomes imperative. In the conflicts on the California streets, we have confronted a watershed of anger, frustration, fear, and alienation. In Western Europe the scapegoating of Mediterranean peoples and resurgent anti-Semitism are becoming too serious to ignore. In these developments we find echoes of centuries-old divisions between ethnic groups, tribes, and castes in other parts of the world. Having left behind the Cold War, the third world war of the twentieth century, events point to a period of ethnic wars around the world, true wars of emotion. In them we can discover the dark side of cultural particularism and the horrifying implications of ethnic isolationism. In our own local contexts, cultural and ethnic labelling may become increasingly popular, leading to the projection of social frustration to specific cultural groups. Simultaneously, people's own groups may be viewed as "the norm." In these developments cultural identity conflicts within persons and interethnic strife and suspicion find a painful meeting point.

The distinctiveness persons of different backgrounds bring to their encounters carry disadvantages as well as opportunities. How people experience their distinctiveness depends on whether they are willing to recognize themselves in others or elect to distance and separate themselves.

This book proposes to balance respect for the rich cultural variety of people seeking help with a celebration of their unique journeys as individuals between cultures in a pluralistic society. Caregivers who reach out effectively across cultural boundaries choose to be enriched, as well as to facilitate the birth of enriching insight. They recognize and value both the otherness and the similarity of the persons they minister to. The overemphasis of otherness could lead to an unnecessary widening of the interpersonal gap, while underlining similarities could result in glossing over of personal uniqueness and distinctiveness.

The cross-cultural caregiver's experiences may encompass both rejection and acceptance. At best, persons and their caregivers will register a meeting of minds and hearts. At worst the caregiver can face a wall of mistrust that sits cemented on the foundations of disappointment and bitterness. The caregiver may be approached with high expectation or receive the benefit of the doubt, or may merely be considered worth another look as a helper from a different background.

First the goal of pastoral care in cross-cultural settings needs to be established. The departure point of this book is the idea that cross-cultural pastoral care must aim to encourage persons away from brokenness and toward wholeness in all areas of their lives. Wholeness ideally would include reconciliation and the restoration of communication in personal relations, acceptance of one's own talents and shortcomings, integration of one's value system-in-process, a harmonious experience of one's faith, as well as behavior consistent with one's self-concept, values, faith, and the nature of one's relationships. In counseling *some* of these issues are always examined, but in cross-cultural pastoral care and counseling *all* these issues in their interconnectedness should be of concern. New strands may be added to care seekers' experience in counseling, but the emphasis should remain on bringing all the elements in their lives together in relative harmony, not on highlighting specific aspects of experience. In cross-cultural pastoral care and counseling, the notion of the unity of experience is fundamental: feelings, thought processes, motivation, behavior, social systems, and value systems all come together in processes. A basic understanding of these dynamics is a prerequisite to effective cross-cultural pastoral care and counseling.

I consider pastoral counseling to be a more in-depth, technical aspect of pastoral care, which is more general, flexible with regard to setting, and relatively short-term. All of the discussions in this book are meant to be useful to pastoral counseling but will also tend to be relevant to pastoral care in general. To simplify matters, I will not distinguish between the two from here on out and will use the terms interchangeably.

This book consists of three main sections. Chapters 1 and 2 form one section highlighting the basic issues of awareness and skills. Chapters 3-6 make up the second section focusing on the three diagnostic categories in cross-cultural pastoral care and counseling and ways of integrating them. The final section consists of relatively brief explorations of specific questions, namely, the use of biblical stories, family pastoral care, care and counseling of specific cultural groups, and pastoral caregiver self-assessment.

1

FUNDAMENTAL AWARENESS

James Kim is a twenty-year-old college student of Korean descent who has come to see his pastor, Susan Brown, a European American. Susan and James have known each other for four years now, and James was active in the senior youth group of the church. There were four other Korean American young people in that group. James finished high school in the top of his class but has not done so well in college. This has caused conflicts with his parents, first generation American citizens, who have worked their way up from being poor immigrants to the upper-middle stratum of society. Their expectations of James, their only son among three children, are high, and James is very much aware of these expectations. He is burdened by the tension between his parents' wishes, which he sees as logical, and his own desire to become a journalist.

James's father is one of the pillars of Susan's congregation, and she has a good relationship with him, albeit a rather reserved and formal one. Susan knows that lately he has been attending services of a new Korean speaking congregation that is applying for membership in her denomination.

Since Susan and James have not met for a while, Susan invites him to lunch, and afterwards James reluctantly begins speaking about his problems with his parents. Susan reacts emotionally by affirming James's right and duty to listen to his own inner voice and even says that she considers his wish to become a journalist to be a calling. She engages in self-disclosure by explaining that she once rebelled against her parents' wishes by becoming a minister, and that now they were "enormously" proud of her, thus making the point that "rebellion can be a normal part of growing up."

At first James seems very pleased by her statements, which appeared to motivate him to talk more about his frustrations:

"Yeah, it's like they see me as an instrument. As if I am in this world to make them look good."

Susan: "You feel used."

James: "Yes, I do. Hey, I don't want to be an engineer. Math bores me. I love ideas, events, telling the truth."

Susan: "And you've always been a great writer."

James: "Thanks, Susan. I guess I need to hear that."

But not much later, James became quieter, and the pastoral conversation turned into a social conversation about what had happened to the other members of the youth group. When they said goodbye, Susan felt something was not right, that perhaps she had taken James's side too much and not adequately acknowledged the complexity of the situation. It was as if by supporting his decision, she had created even greater turmoil.

The relationship between Susan and James has always been good, characterized by mutual liking and respect. James enjoyed being "American" with Susan. He did not have to worry about the expectations of his family, which he saw as limiting his expression. Somehow he never felt he could be truly himself at home, for there was a "goofy" side to him his parents would not approve of. He was always putting on his good and obedient face at home and among his parents' friends. But on the other hand, being "American," being free to express himself, did not feel totally right either. He realized that he tried too much to fit in sometimes, forcing himself to adapt perfectly to yet another culture. While in the Korean community he often felt suppressed, in a European American setting he sometimes felt fake. Susan was quite supportive, emphasizing his personal freedom and his unique talents, and that helped James, but she did not quite recognize the ambivalence James carried with him. At times he wanted to be the true Korean son, the accomplished academic with a bright career in medicine or engineering in front of him, but he also had the desire to beat European Americans at being American by succeeding in fields his people avoided by instinct.

Susan is tempted to see James as any student dealing with authoritarian, controlling parents. But she misses the point by doing so. On a parental scale within the Korean community, James's parents may not be authoritarian at all. They merely follow tradition, acting out of their own fear of poverty, deference to their ancestors, and love for their son. So perhaps Susan's assurance that rebellion can be an appropriate part of growing up is very much out of line, and at some level James may know that. If he believes he is asking Susan to condone rebellion against his parents, that may evoke quite a bit of guilt on his part, for they have always acted like loving Korean parents, practicing what their parents preached before them.

This mistake and a number of others can be avoided or kept to a minimum through a number of categories of awareness to cross-cultural pastoral care and counseling outlined below.

THE UNITY OF EXPERIENCE

James's story illustrates how emotional, social, and cultural aspects become intertwined. However, when caregivers treat persons, they do not always demonstrate awareness of such dynamics. The temptation to analyze problems through the lens of only one discipline is great. In pastoral care and counseling, the overwhelming influence on analytical methods and intervention comes from counseling psychology. Counseling methodology is usually only partially informed by experience and largely based on general theories of personality (cf. Sue and Sue 1990, 137–38). These theories of personality constitute philosophical assumptions on which caregivers base their methodology. This can be a dangerous undertaking, for these philosophical assumptions are culturally determined, meaning they were born in the interaction between scholars and their own cultural environment. Caregivers choose personality theories on the basis of the education they received, their cultural experience, their professional experience, and their own personality type. This means that their methodology is largely arrived at through deductive means. I am suggesting that we shift from predominantly deductive to predominantly inductive reasoning to arrive at a caregiving methodology or methodologies. This means that the experience of the person needing care becomes the starting point of the caregiver's methodology. As far as possible, the counselor must set aside the assumptions of the counseling method used. One must avoid falling into the trap of limiting one's diagnosis only to the caregiver's traditional area of interest, namely the psychological and perhaps the spiritual. Human experience is dynamic and interconnected, involving intrapsychic processes, interpersonal interaction, socioeconomic factors, faith questions, value judgments, and physical condition. Therefore, the cross-cultural caregiver is encouraged to be conscious of the different processes that are impacting on each other in the care seeker's life.

Closely related are the types of culture that have bearing on human experience. As we will discover further on, persons all carry and operate with dominant and less dominant cultures. European societies in general have made the individual the focus of their cultural understanding, so many customs, rules, and rituals in those societies are clustered around the notion of a person's rights, responsibility, and freedom. These cultures have been referred to by Shweder and Bourne as "egocentric," favoring the individual over the community (Shweder and LeVine 1984, 187–95). Over against this type of culture are set "holistic" cultures, which tend to be "sociocentric," emphasizing the community over the individual. Shweder and Bourne use the human body as a metaphor to describe the second type, referring to holistic cultures as "organic," while the egocentric type is considered "contractual." One's primary culture may be egocentric while one's secondary culture is sociocentric. This is true of James, whose individualistic American culture clashes with his traditional familial culture.

AWARENESS OF EXPECTATIONS

Not all persons seeking helping across cultural boundaries will come with the same expectations. However, someone who takes the step to seek help through cross-cultural pastoral care will probably have high expectations. This is often true of Asians. Many Asians may not react favorably to predominantly client-centered approaches that stress mirroring over interpretation and directiveness. They will have been raised with the notion that helping means prescribing behavior instead of accompanying a person on the road to new perspectives and behaviors.

"Attractiveness" and "trustworthiness" have been identified as central attributes for counselors in cross-cultural settings (Sue and Sue 1990, 81–92). Attractiveness is determined in reference to one or more

variables the care seeker identifies in the caregiver. These variables include the following psychological sets: problem solving, consistency,
identity, authority, and finally, economic mindset. Persons with a problem solving set will choose a caregiver because they believe he or she
can solve or help solve their problems. Consistency means that what the
caregiver expresses is consistent with the care seeker's own values and
beliefs. The identity set urges someone to look for a helping professional with a similar cultural background. Persons *in* authority are attractive to persons with an authority set. The economic set motivates
persons to seek help from persons who can deliver a form of reward or
punishment (Sue and Sue 1990, 83–87).

An awareness of what makes a caregiver attractive to a person seeking
help can be very helpful in understanding why the care seeker acts a certain way. I have found that the problem solving set is encountered most
frequently in Asia, but consistency and identity are also very significant.
The economic mindset does not appear to be as common.

For James, identity is important, since both he and his pastor share
the life of the church. Perhaps authority is also important, for the opinion of the pastor is very important in Korean culture. The trouble in
James's encounter with Susan lies in the area of consistency, for a gap
exists between the values of James' parents and those of the pastor. Susan's pastoral ability for problem solving is not what drew James to
Susan as caregiver, and her attempt to solve James's problems in fact
trivialized his dilemma. This helps explain why Susan was only partially
effective, even though James would not think of calling her trustworthiness into question. Susan as a caregiver was attractive and credible to
James because she accepted the part of him his parents found difficult
to accept.

A word of caution with regard to these sets. Persons are very complex and they are always in transitions. They are apt to defy labels and
categories. Therefore these categories should not be applied rigidly.

AWARENESS OF GENDER ROLES

The roles of men and women, especially of women, vary greatly from
one primary culture to another. On the road to self-actualization, the
degree to which a caregiver can help raise the consciousness of a care
seeker regarding gender may differ significantly from one situation to

another. The caregiver should be realistic about how far and how fast a person can travel on the road to greater gender awareness. High caregiver expectations may frustrate both caregiver and care seeker.

For James, the pressure to excel in engineering or medicine was increased by the fact that he was the male who inherits the responsibility for becoming a good provider. In most cultures gender roles are gradually changing, and the available ways to express a sense of liberation are also changing. We can express liberation in different spheres, such as employment, personal relationships, expression of feelings, and the way we choose to dress. Caregivers will find that for women in many countries, because of different tolerance levels, sexism is not or not yet the emotional issue it is in North America. This may frustrate the caregiver who is dedicated to broadening the horizons of the care seeker. Caregivers should therefore lower their expectations. As James can be hurt by a well-meaning Susan who calls into question the values of his parents' culture, so a woman from a different cultural background can be made to feel alienated from her primary culture when the caregiver dismisses the way men and women relate in that culture. Even though the grounds for such intervention may be ethically sound and therapeutically responsible in North American cultural settings, it may deepen certain crises instead of relieving them. It may be helpful to operate with an informal awareness scale between very high "identity suppression and role oppression" and very low "identity suppression and role oppression" when cross-culturally counseling women, as well as men, with reference to the different spheres of expression I just mentioned. When tackling gender issues, the objective should be to help the care seeker move toward the nonoppressive end of the scale in a way that does not violate the integrity of the diagnostic categories yet to be discussed.

AWARENESS OF CULTURAL CODES

In cross-cultural communication an awareness of cultural communication codes can remove certain obstacles to understanding. These codes are not always discernable, for language does not always lift the veil. Language is a process that connects meanings with words, signs, sounds. But especially in cross-cultural communication, it is not always effective. Codes inform our language.

Four categories of cultural codes are often referred to when explaining cross-cultural communication. Category A consists of cultural codes that are implicit and limited to the group in a group-oriented society that emphasizes social roles. Category B codes extend beyond the group and are explicit in a group-oriented society emphasizing roles. Category C codes are group-limited but implicit in a person-oriented society. Finally, category D covers cultural codes extending beyond the group that are explicit in a person-oriented society. We can find category A, for example, in many Asian societies. Category B can be found in a traditional, community-oriented society that has been able or been forced to communicate with the outside world. Close-knit cultural groups within the United States would generally fall in category C, while the primary culture of North Americans can generally be found in category D. For A the main values are *piety* and *sense of honor*; for B, *duty*; for C, *genuineness* and *dependability*; and for D, *self-actualization* and *altruism*. From A to D the spectrum runs from emphasis on *form* to emphasis on *contents* (Douglas 1973).

If we take these categories seriously, we can conclude that with certain care seekers, caregivers would face a significantly wider gap than with others because of the nature of the codes, for people tend to carry their worldview or cognitive structures into conversation.

Chances are that the cultural codes of James's father can mostly be found in category A, in spite of his many years in North America. But again it must be noted that the cultures of persons are in process, and therefore so are their cultural codes. James's communication may be informed by codes that fall in a number of categories. Therefore it is best that the caregiver be aware of these codes but not employ them rigidly as analytical tools.

OTHER RELIGIONS

Pastoral caregivers might be biased toward their own faith and often will consider it to be of universal significance. But quite often those who seek help across cultures are adherents of other religious traditions. This can create a dilemma for caregivers, for they may consider aspects of the care seeker's religion to be oppressive or deviant from the truth. The caregiver is stuck between respect and sensitivity on the one hand, and personal conviction on the other. This is not a dilemma the caregiver is likely to become comfortable with. Caregivers with a more universalist approach to religions, which allows them to accept the truth of those religions, or caregivers who see their religious faith as exclusively true will be less troubled by this dilemma than the majority who find themselves between those two positions. I have found it helpful to remember that, as anthropologists often remind us, religion and culture are inseparable. Religion is, in fact, part of culture and is to be treated respectfully as culture.

In a helping context, pastoral care and counseling may not be restricted to persons with the same religious backgrounds. While the caregiver will operate, of course, with great sensitivity to the worldview of care seekers with a different religious background, care seekers will rarely offend the religious sensibilities of the caregiver, for caregivers will already be aware of the religious differences. If, however, caregivers at any point feel compromised in their own beliefs, it will suffice to say, "I must let you know that from the point of view of my faith, I look at this question differently, but I am trying to understand what this means to you." If the problem presented by care seekers is very much a theological question only answerable within their own religious tradition, it may be better to refer them to a religious functionary acknowledged by that group as officially adhering to that tradition.

Interestingly, care seekers who have rejected the ancient traditions of other religions in favor of the Christian faith are most adverse to the idea of openness to the rejected tradition. The caregiver must understand that many of these people, or their parents, had to suffer the rejection of their relatives and perhaps a whole community when they changed their faith. Such a radical change and the suffering it entailed makes what seems to them to be "glossing over" theological differences hard to swallow. For them lines must be clearly drawn, and to brush over them in an attempt to be culturally tolerant could be a therapeutic mistake on the part of the caregiver. For example, James may be intrigued with the Confucian tradition of Korea. He was born in the United States and old traditions hold no painful memories for him, but to his parents Confucianism may have different associations because they view the tradition in a blur of painful childhood memories that have very little to do with religion but a great deal to do with family relationships. It is important to understand that for a person to move from one religion to another may result in a complete breakdown of relationships with the original belonging group.

SOCIAL CLASS AND STATUS

In most countries some form of social stratification can be found. But it is important that the caregiver realizes a class issue may play a role in any problem. American society is generally not as much a class-oriented society as a race-oriented society. Many North Americans value a person who moves up from one class to another, and movies often bestow the epithet of hero to the person who perseveres and succeeds. Thus the contempt people of many cultural groups feel toward members of another class is often quite baffling to the American caregiver. For instance, one could speak near perfect Vietnamese with a well-educated person from North Vietnam, yet a single wrong word could affect one's reputation for life in the eyes of the conversation partner.

Class is often expressed in language. The Javanese language, for example, consists of three almost completely different languages in one. The lowest level is spoken between friends and to children or subordinates; and the middle level, between respected equals or persons one does not know well. The highest level is reserved for highly respected elders and high officials. Javanese from the hinterlands can be quite nervous about speaking the two highest levels of their own language, often preferring the more egalitarian and truly pluralistic national language, Bahasa Indonesia, which is made up of a Malay core, Sanskrit words, Arabic for the whole spectrum of religious terms, some Portuguese words adopted centuries ago, and then Dutch for pre-1950 technical terms. It is easy to mix up the Javanese language levels, and doing so betrays one's lower position in society.

It is important for caregivers not to view these stratifications as justifying their prejudices toward the cultures of care seekers, but as a sign of how alien these care seekers feel within the groups they consider as other, their sense of alienation instilled through centuries of cultural programming. It is also crucial to remember that in many societies, the financial resources or the space to distance oneself from other people do not exist as they do in North America, so stratification is also used to separate one's group from others.

Particularly in Latin America, the differences in class are visible in the extreme contrasts between the rich and the poor, which have led to a violent struggle for freedom from economic oppression. The caregiver should be aware of the scars these struggles have left in care seekers who may have had family members killed or disappeared or who have been tortured. The emotional processes that have resulted may be too much for the caregiver to handle, and referral to a more skilled and trained caregiver is recommended with severe cases.

Class and cultural differences reinforce each other, and in many ways class differences are cultural differences, for in both the language and the habits are distinct. Within James's Korean American community, new class differences could easily emerge between the new more conservative immigrants who are struggling financially, and the acculturated, bilingual Korean Americans who have reached a higher level of financial security.

INTERGENERATIONAL TENSIONS

In more ways than one the generations represent cultures of their own. This is definitely true of Korean culture. Each generation in its middle years feels it has earned the right to be in power, and when the chance finally comes, members of each generation are ready to exert it. This is true in many sectors of society. Over the last decades, the younger generation has been begun to challenge the power of the elders, and this trend is bound to continue. The generational tension to a certain degree plays a role in James's problem, and the caregiver should be cautious not to heighten this tension unnecessarily.

A DYNAMIC UNDERSTANDING OF CULTURE

Cultural anthropologists, particularly those who emphasize the central role of symbol in culture, often give *meaning* a central place in their definition of culture. They see culture as "an historically transmitted pattern of meanings embodied in symbols" (Shweder and LeVine 1984, 1), "meaning systems" (Shweder and LeVine 1984, 111), or "knowledge, meaning and symbols" (Shweder and LeVine 1984, 20). Their argument for organizing the definition around meaning is that everything that makes culture produces meaning for those who are influenced by that culture. Rituals, customs, values, beliefs all produce meaning. Culture exists by virtue of the meaning it produces for people by way of values, beliefs and rituals, as well as customs and other types of behavior. For example, status and profession hold a different meaning for Susan than they do for James's father.

Not all anthropologists share the preoccupation with meaning, for a large number are more interested in the function of beliefs, customs, rituals, and the like, in a particular society or community, or in how relationships are structured in a society or group. These are valid emphases in the exploration of cultures, but they are less useful in the study of individual interactions in a pluralistic society that is fluid and changeable.

Traditionally, anthropologists have focused their research on cultures that are relatively isolated and untouched by the surrounding world. Not only are these cultures increasingly rare, but members of the groups belonging to these cultures are not likely to seek assistance from a caregiver with a different cultural background. Therefore such research is limited in its relevance for cross-cultural pastoral care.

Many anthropologists tend to focus on "patterns." This implies a less dynamic view, that social interaction is recurring rather than developing in new directions. However, culture is never static but constantly in process. Therefore I will be stressing the concept of culture as process.

The culture and personality school in anthropology, including such famous scholars as Margaret Mead and Ruth Benedict (for example, Benedict 1989), discerned an analogy between personality and culture. Thus a personality type could also become a cultural type. This makes it possible for us to speak of the personality of Korean Americans, for example. Such insight is helpful because we can detect parallels between persons and cultures. For example, just as it makes sense to argue that persons and the cultures within them are in process, so we can argue that cultures in general are in process. Yet these parallel processes are not synchronized at all times, because culture does not develop in a vacuum. For instance, members of Korean American culture groups interact with members of other groups with varying intensity and frequency. While Korean American culture changes, the rate and nature of the changes will vary from one person to another. Nevertheless, a correlation exists between societal culture and an individual's orientation.

Cultures are in flux for both caregiver and care receiver, as well for in the groups and society within which they live, but the culture changes are not always simultaneous. The opportunity for getting to know the other's world is minimal, so the caregiver's efforts must be based on a sound understanding of the dynamics within these processes, which shall be discussed.

Consistency will be served if culture is seen wholistically, both in terms of individuals and in terms of larger society, for earlier the commitment to treating persons wholistically was stressed. This has consequences for the way we define culture. A wholistic view of persons implies our willingness to cross boundaries created by labels and categorizations. We must strive to avoid allowing our understandings to be determined by categorizations. As persons are freed up more to be from many worlds and to move toward new worlds, a flexible concept of culture must be employed, allowing reflections about the cultures of caregivers and care seekers to be determined by their experience, not by rigid categories. Thus a concept of culture as *meaning providing processes determined and perpetuated by a group* is appropriate. This concept covers categories utilized by anthropologists such as beliefs, values, ritual, customs, and other types of behavior.

The idea of clear cultural boundaries to delineate the cultures of persons has already been rejected. This has somewhat perplexing implications. We should not attempt to label someone as Mexican American or Arab American or Korean American, since that might negate the additional cultural influences in that person's life. But does this not make cultural differentiations rather troublesome, if not impossible? Generally in a pluralistic context, the focus cannot be on counseling or caregiving to "Latino Americans" or "African Americans." The Latino American may be married to the African American or have many friends from the other community. What we can do is speak of *primary cultural backgrounds.* James's primary cultural background is Korean American, and his mother's is Korean. That does give Susan a cognitive framework of some kind through which to evaluate James's thoughts, feelings, and behavior, while not denying the complexity and changeable nature of his cultural experience.

We could now claim that all caregiving is potentially cross-cultural. Perhaps this is the proper perspective on pastoral care and counseling in pluralistic societies such as in North America. Different religious groups really have different ways of relating, acting, and speaking, thus employing different *meaning providing processes*. Nowadays nearly everyone watches television, and so many channels are available that people become virtual subscribers to particular channels, while never watching any of the others. These channels feature programs with their own language, ritual, and behavior. To a certain degree the meaning providing processes are distinct. This brings us to another question of boundaries, namely the boundary between culture and what is often called "subculture." The distinction between the two may be useful in anthropological research, but again it is too rigid for caregiving purposes.

In summary, the following principle should be stressed: The caregiver must be actively sensitive to the interrelated processes at work in the life of care seeker, the expectations of the caregiver in a particular encounter, the care seeker's place on a gender role and identity awareness scale, the variations within cultural codes, the manifestation of class differences, the possibility of other religious worldviews emerging in the interaction, the influence of intergenerational tensions as a result of cultural traditions, and the nature of culture as processes that provide meaning.

2

ESSENTIAL SKILLS

On a wintry afternoon George van Buren, the European American pastor of a medium-size congregation in a predominantly European American suburb, is told by his secretary that he has a visitor. George has been feeling tired, and after debating whether to work on his sermon or go visit a chronically ill member in the hospital, he has just decided to open up his file of sermon illustrations. Suddenly he is introduced by his secretary to a woman from Ethiopia who wishes to speak to the pastor. George is not fond of situations where strangers walk into the church. He is quite certain the conversation will lead to a request for money, and he is just not very good in these circumstances. He wants to help people, for that desire helped lead him into the ministry in the first place. On the other hand, he does not want to be used as a source of easy money. Consequently, when people come to ask for financial assistance, he feels dissatisfied when he agrees to help, but also uncomfortable when he declines. Therefore, when the North African woman, Asmarat, sat down on the couch in his study, he was already ill-disposed toward her.

However, his attitude changed swiftly as he began to realize that she, although of little means, did not come for financial support but to search for a community. Asmarat, a native of the country of Eritrea (until recently a region of Ethiopia), had been very active in the Ethiopian Church in Addis Ababa, a church with a great history. Her husband, feeling that as an Eritrean nationalist he would have no future in Ethiopia, applied for refugee status in the United States. Asmarat and her children followed. A strong woman, she found odd jobs to support the family as her husband sank into a deep depression. He blamed the depression on the injury he had sustained while fighting Ethiopian government troups. The injury had been so severe that a small part of his skull was replaced with synthetic material. After a few glasses of beer, he would enjoy having people touch the spot and watching them recoil in fright. He once told Asmarat that it made him feel a bit heroic. But their marriage went from bad to worse, until finally Asmarat moved to another state two thousand miles away. She rented an apartment and moved in with her two children. George was one of the first persons she met in her new domicile. Her connection point was the church, although she and George did not have the same theological background. She believed that her active role in the church back home would be a passport to a new family, while George was steadying himself to reject another "walk-in looking for a hand-out."

Her story transformed George's attitude. It changed his attitude from cold to empathetic, for it was clear that she wanted a brother, not money. George tried very hard to make her welcome in the congregation, even introducing her to the choir director. Over time, Asmarat stopped coming to church and George lost touch with her, but not before she had given him an Ethiopian cross and had baked him several loaves of large flat Ethiopian bread.

ATTENDING SKILLS

Most trained caregivers have been taught to utilize attending skills such as listening, body language, visual communication, and simple brief verbal responses. Attending skills will vary from one person to the other, depending on such factors as cultural background, gender, and age. Native Americans tend to prefer to have a desk between themselves and the caregiver, something most pastoral care trainers would discourage (Sue 1981, 216–48). The same is true of most Asians. Physical proximity is often more threatening than comforting, especially if the caregiver is male and the person seeking care is female. The physical proximity will become the emotional focus of the encounter instead of a soothing background of acceptance. This problem is often referred to as "space preference" (Dillard 1983, 285–314).

Equal height in seating is important. In general, it is probably wise to have all persons present seated on chairs of equal height and quality, with a low table or other large low object placed between the caregiver and the other person or persons present.

Eye contact is another question that needs attention. In most European cultures, constant or near constant eye contact is important in communicating respect, but this is not often the case with other cultural groups. The Javanese in Indonesia avoid direct eye contact almost exclusively in one-to-one encounters. First generation Chinese Americans often prefer short periods of eye contact followed by moments of eye contact avoidance. African Americans are generally not appreciative of constant eye contact. But then there are cultural groups, such as the Batak in Indonesia, who almost demand eye contact as a way of being shown respect. They may be angered by eye contact avoidance. In case the caregiver has no clue about the frequency and length of eye contact, it is probably wise to alternate contact with focusing on a point on the wall, for example, that is about at the persons's eye level. Usually if eye contact disturbs them, care receivers will give caregivers clues for instance, looking toward the floor more frequently.

Body posture also varies greatly from one culture to another. Crossing the legs is generally not considered polite. In some Indonesian cultures, placing the hands on the hips with elbows bent is considered offensive, as is showing the bottom of the feet in Thai cultures. Also, never receive any object with the left hand as many Asians, among others, will be offended by that.

Many Asians find it offensive if, when waving for someone to come, a person uses one finger with the palm facing upward. It is more acceptable to face the right hand downward and wave all fingers simultaneously. At all costs, avoid pointing the finger at the care seeker when making a point.

It is best to assume that hugging is inappropriate, although this will vary according with the length of time a person has spent among North Americans. If hugging is considered appropriate, it is probably more often acceptable among women or as a way of greeting and saying goodbye. Warm, extraverted persons are not necessarily huggers. If the caregiver finds this to be an essential part of his or her ministry, it can be discussed with the care seeker. Holding the hand of a person who is distraught is often quite appropriate.

Americans are the most eager of all people to relate to anyone on a first-name basis. Even the French and the Dutch, for example, always need to establish first in any relationship whether a less formal way of addressing the other is deemed appropriate. Therefore, it is preferable to always address adults with Mr., Mrs. or Miss until they give the green light for a different way of addressing. Although using someone's first name can warm a relationship, in cross-cultural communication, it can be quite awkward when done too quickly.

Nodding is usually quite an appropriate way of attending, but one needs to know that slight, backward-directed nods can mean disapproval in some cultures. Therefore it is important that a nodding movement be accompanied with facial expressions showing sincerity, interest, and compassion.

Shaking the head may have different connotations. Persons with primary cultures originating from the Indian subcontinent and Sri Lanka often sway their heads, as if they were disagreeing with something. However, they can be in complete agreement when doing so. I have found that the gesture can express self-consciousness or emotion of any kind.

Asmarat clearly appreciated the warmth and caring George communicated after the first awkward moments. In other cultures this behavior might have been misread as being sexual in nature. To Asmarat, who comes from a rather open, extraverted culture, this was perfectly natural. George once visited her at her apartment when she was there alone. In some cultures, for a male alone to go to a woman's house with no one else present would be unwise, but in this case the pastoral relationship progressed as it would with a European American.

RESPONDING SKILLS

Beyond nonverbal responses, such as nodding, eye contact, and so forth, and simple verbal responses such as "I see" and "oh really" that witness to the caregiver's alertness and focus, significant verbal responses of course need to be appropriate also. One difficulty can be varied understandings of the word "feel" or "feeling." In many languages these terms may have a much wider connotation, including meanings such as "opinion" and "interpretation." Therefore if the pastor asks "how do do you feel about that," a whole range of cognitive responses may ensue. One other way the caregiver can approach someone's feeling is by using empathy, for instance "I hear you saying you feel hurt." One must remember that sentences such as these, however accurate they may be, are part of a special counseling language often not understood by care seekers or when understood may alienate them. So often these kinds of statement sound contrived in a cross-cultural care setting. The caregiver must find a way to express caring and understanding, and thus encourage self-expression and awareness of feelings, without widening the already significant cultural gap. Undoubtedly the caring one communicates by being there with this person and listening, and reacting with his or her own life will motivate and warm the care seeker. But through skills and awareness, pastors can enhance what is already being accomplished through their basic caring.

I have found it useful to make empathetic responses rather quickly and "between the lines," using statements such as "I'm sorry to hear that," "that must be really hard," or "how painful." Appropriate empathetic facial expressions should, of course, accompany the words. In many cross-cultural care contexts, attending skills and genuineness will outweigh the responding skills in their effectiveness. Pastoral counselors with large case loads may want to keep that in mind and schedule their cross-cultural appointments during times of the day when they are not overly tired or feel particularly drained.

It is important to note that persons from a different cultural background will often have to overcome reluctance to discuss their personal problems. Seeing a pastoral counselor may be especially foreign to their primary culture. Approaching a pastor or priest is more acceptable, but embarrassment or guilt may be more of an obstacle in that setting. Any gesture from the caregiver that might create an impression of disinterest or irritation may close the door permanently to the counseling relationship.

The caregiver will be able to request clarification or further information in most situations without offending the care seeker. However, in an effort to be concrete, the caregiver should be careful not to cross the line between concreteness and confrontation when addressing apparent contradictions or lack of cooperation. Also, the idea of a contract between caregiver and care seeker should also not be overly emphasized, because cultural interpretations concerning whether the contract is being adhered to by either or both of the parties are likely to differ.

There is no telling how a person will react to us as caregivers. Some will be completely unaccustomed to empathy. Perhaps no one has ever identified with care seeker's feelings. This was to a certain degree the case with Asmarat. She comes from a poor country where everyone is struggling to survive, and her people were at war with Ethiopia for decades. There was no time for the sensitivities of everyday living there. On the other hand, an Asian person I met with reacted with great irritation when I looked down for a few seconds in reflection. She assumed I was looking at my watch and wished to hint to her that I wanted her to leave.

LANGUAGE SKILLS

Many persons who seek help across cultures have a limited command of English. This may not be apparent at first. North Americans are quite accustomed to people with regional or foreign accents, so the care seeker's difficulty in expressing himself or herself is often overlooked. The caregiver may see the person as shy or introverted. But speaking a foreign language is often frightening. I remember an American church official reporting on the Spanish language course he had taken in Costa Rica and explaining how difficult it had been for him. At one point he exclaimed that the new immigrants who must learn English were heroes for mastering a new language. The more we age, the harder it is to learn a new language.

Learning a new language is not only technically difficult but can also be emotionally draining. A person mastering a new language may spend years being laughed at by native speakers. But there are many issues a new speaker has to deal with. For instance, in Indonesian the following words are similar: "teach" and "chase," "sin" and "prayer," "wind" and "dog." And think about how difficult it would be for someone learning English to distinguish between "to," "two," and "too," or between "write" and "right," or "wide" and "white." Many nonnative speakers find English hard because it is not written as it sounds. ("To know" sounds like "too no.") Many Asian languages, like Cantonese and Vietnamese, depend heavily on tones. This whole tonal reservoir of meanings and subtleties becomes useless in English where, for instance, the important difference between plural and singular or past and present is expressed by changing the form of the noun or verb. (In Indonesian the plural is formed by repeating a singular word.) Then there is the difference between passive and active language. Some languages make greater use of passive forms, where the emphasis is put on the object or the victim of the action, while in active forms, more common in English, the subject is the primary focus.

In languages with similar roots to English, another problem emerges. Words may look very similar but have different meanings. For example, the verb "acostar" in Spanish means "putting someone to bed," not "to accost." "Agonia" does not mean "agony" but is instead associated with one's last breath before passing away. Some terms, which may seem fairly ordinary to native English speakers may be a source of great sensitivity, such as the Spanish term "abuela," or grandmother. In Latino cultures mothers and grandmothers are approached with great reverence, and using the term can be a source of great offense. Thus even a Latino American who speaks English quite well may have emotional associations with certain words.

Most caregivers in the United States and a great many in Canada are not fluent in a language other then English, for they do not have to be. In this regard, they do not differ from the Australians, New Zealanders, British, or French, and they are less aware of the expressions a person may or may not understand. I suggest that caregivers develop their cross-cultural language skills by thinking of the words and expressions we would most want to know when learning another language. Nouns, of course, are critical. We would then want to learn simple verbs, without worrying too much about how the verbs would change. Then perhaps we would add the pronouns and prepositions. To speakers of English as a foreign language, these same things are important. They focus on the simple words that help them communicate. A caregiver, instead of saying "So do you see yourself as a friendly person generally?" could say to a person with very limited English proficiency, "To you, are you friendly?" That way segements of the sentence are conveniently separated. Another example might be: "Whenever you have an idea, do you tend to run with it?" This is a day-to-day North American expression that almost any native speaker would understand. But it is a football metaphor. More simply one could say "When you have an idea, a thought, what do you do?" It is helpful to gesture, so that, for example, size, intensity, and duration can be apparent to the caregiver. In extreme cases, a caregiver could even keep the verbs to the minimum, using terse sentences: "Your husband, to you, he is good." Of course, the caregiver should be extremely cautious not to talk down to the care seeker. Simplifying one's language beyond the point needed for communication will be insulting.

In urban neighborhhoods in many countries, including in North America, new language understood only by its users tends to be developed by young people, many of them from minority groups. The caregiver should not pretend to know this language but should show an interest in learning and not hesitate to let the care receiver who uses this language become a teacher.

Caregivers should be aware of where persons learned their English. Americans, Canadians, New Zealanders, Australians, English, the Scots, and the Irish routinely ridicule each other's speech and vocabulary with a smile, but where a nonnative speaker of English has learned to speak the language is definitely a factor to be aware of. The same word can have very different meanings. For instance, a great many English speaking people "collect" their children at school, but that sense would mystify most United States residents. Also a word like "horrid" does not have as strong a meaning in most places as it does in North America.

When care seekers have a limited command of English, it may be best to avoid altogether expressions such as "killing two birds with one stone" or "you feel you're getting burned again" or "sleeping like a log."

In addition, caregivers should not forget that they easily fall into cliches such as "getting in touch with your feelings" and "finding out who you are" and "are we connecting?" To many care seekers from minority cultures who do know the language well, these will be alienating expressions of the majority culture that suggest a lack of genuineness and a lack of willingness to make new language together. Instead, caregivers should search for metaphors that are fresh or expressive of the care seeker's experience, metaphors that are cross-culturally relevant. For instance, one could say "It is as if your emotions are like a wild horse: when it wants to run, you cannot control it"; or "you are so sensitive right now that criticism is like ice on a sore tooth." In every culture, such metaphors would be understood.

Asmarat had a relatively good understanding of the language, but was not able to understand expressions such as the ones just mentioned. Language had to be literal, and she was unable to distinguish cliches from relatively fresh language. People generally understand more than they can express in words. This was true of Asmarat, whose sentences were short. When expressing their emotions, people's words often get in the way of rather than facilitate the transfer of meaning.

HERMENEUTICAL SKILLS

The task ahead is to build on the groundwork of awareness and skills, to add content to the form discussed above. Although the genuine caring of pastors; their awareness of codes, expectations, and consistency, and their utilization of specific skills will narrow the gap between caregiver and care seeker, more is needed. The central challenge is to help the caregiver find a way to understand what the life of the care seeker is like, in other words: to empathize. But empathy is not really possible in radically cross-cultural encounters. Empathy is an intentional, conscious act that takes imagination, although the empathizing person recognizes that the experience of the other is not the same. When we "sympathize," our own experience is both "frame and picture." When we empathize, the identifier's experience is the frame, and the experience of the other is the picture. But it is very difficult for someone to grasp the picture of another across cultures. Therefore the concept of *interpathy* needs to be introduced (Augsburger 1986, 31/32). Interpathy is one step further away from sympathy. It is an affective and cognitive intentional act to understand the world of another. While in empathy, the worldviews are still relatively similar, in interpathy a clear gap of understanding is bridged.

The question of *frame of reference* forms the background for this problem. If caregiver and care seeker share frames of reference, that is, the same cultural stories, similar values, similar beliefs, and similar cultural experiences, empathy is more likely to take place. To facilitate interpathy, the experience of the pastor and the experience of the person seeking help must be brought closer together through mutual understanding. Segments of frames of reference must be brought into contact somehow. That is one of the challenges we will address further on: how to set the stage for understanding the other. This involves hermeneutical skill, which is not easily learned and is related to diagnostic skills and all types of awareness discussed so far. Essentially, hermeneutical skills concern the meaning a certain experience has for a care seeker. George learned what the church meant to Asmarat and what it meant to her to be accepted in a new church family, although he probably did not grasp

it fully nor could he put it into words. Yet with hermeneutical skill, perhaps for an instant he was able to cross the line to achieve some kind of
understanding he did not previously have, an understanding compat-
ible with hers. The types of awareness discussed earlier combined with
appropriate attending and responding skills set the stage for hermeneutical skills, which nevertheless can only be guaranteed through experience.

DIAGNOSTIC SKILLS

Diagnostic skills entail the ability to arrive at problem definition from a
cross-culturally valid framework. We will be developing this framework
in the next chapters. A diagnostically skilled caregiver will be capable of
utilizing the cross-culturally valid diagnostic categories without bias or
preconceived stereotypes. These categories are worldview, sense of belonging, and identity, which are dynamically interrelated and in process.
For Asmarat, her worldview, her sense of belonging, and her identity
came together in the church.

INTEGRATIVE SKILLS

Diagnostic skills must be complemented by integrative skills, which
enable caregivers to help care seekers integrate the worldview, identity,
and sense of belonging with changing realities. At all times the exploration of specific issues should lead back to some sort of integration of
the person's self-understanding, understanding of himself or herself in
community, and his or her perception of reality. If there is significant
conflict within these categories or between them, tension and anxiety
are sure to result. For Asmarat, after separating from her church and
husband, regaining a new sense of belonging was an important issue to
which George tried to respond.

METHODOLOGICAL SKILLS

Another set of basic skills for the care giver in cross-cultural communication are methodological in nature. As was said earlier, most experienced caregivers work with certain models. These models consist of
stages of information seeking and intervention and are characterized by

the emphasis on particular skills and techniques. The complexity of the intercultural encounter may compel caregivers to abandon their preferred model, because certain techniques may have an undesirable effect on the growth of the care seeker. Therefore, we need to provide a cross-cultural model that can complement or correct prevalent models for the cross-cultural pastoral care context. The cross-cultural caregiver must realize that being locked into particular therapeutic methods, whether cognitive therapy, client-centered counseling, behavioral methods, or problem solving therapy, is a liability in cross-cultural pastoral care and counseling. I have found that specific cultural, age, and status groups respond well to different approaches, and there is too much variation to make generalizations of any sort. Yet I believe if caregivers can integrate the categories of worldview, identity, and sense of belonging into their primary methodology, the damage to the care seeker can be kept to a minimum. With Asmarat, an emphasis on her feelings worked well, but it was incomplete to the degree that it left the three categories unexplored.

Some of the fundamental skills and types of awareness needed in effective cross-cultural pastoral care and counseling have been presented. This is not intended to be an exhaustive inventory but groundwork for pastoral action.

The discussion above translates in the following set of principles:

- The caregiver should utilize appropriate attending and responding skills to respect interactional preferences
- The caregiver should utilize language in a straightforward way and with appropriate complexity.
- The caregiver should seek to deepen hermeneutical skills.
- The caregiver should practice diagnostic and integrative skills.
- The caregiver should maintain methodological flexibility.

3

ASSESSING WORLDVIEW

Noel is an African American campus minister at a large Christian college. While he is in his office preparing the Sunday chapel service, he is visited by a student couple, the woman, a local European American, the man, a law student from a small island in the Indian Ocean. They introduce themselves as David and Becky, explaining that most people find David's real name hard to pronounce. Noel has seen them a few times as his eyes scanned his small congregation on campus, but has never spoken to them.

They explain that they have fallen in love and wish to be married. However, there is one major obstacle to their wedding plans, namely that David is expected to marry someone else in his home village. Noel, curious, asks the appropriate question: whether David loves the woman he is supposed to marry and whether he loves Becky. David answers adamantly that he loves Becky and not the other woman. In fact, he explains that he has he has only met the other candidate twice, once when they were ten years old and once before he left to finish his studies.

Noel cautiously states that the task before them seems obvious: to inform the original candidate that David is forced to break the engagement, as difficult as that may be. Although respectful of other cultures, Noel reacts from his own experience to this tradition, which to him is oppressive. To him, everyone should have the freedom to move anywhere, be anybody, and love anyone, a right he feels was and is so often denied to African Americans. Becky then tells Noel the consequences of such an action, namely that David's widowed mother, who holds a prominent position in his village, will lose face in front of the prospective bride's family, as well as the entire community. David faces a dilemma of love, forced to choose between his love and respect for his mother and his love for Becky. Moreover, David's mother has been diagnosed as being terminally ill and has made the strongest of appeals for David to marry prior to her passing.

Noel asks: "How do you feel about this, Becky?"

Becky: "I feel sorry for David. He's such a good man and I can see this is really tearing him apart. Why should he have to marry someone he doesn't love? I mean, he is really concerned about what our marriage would do to his village, and I understand he can't just throw everything away, but do they care about his happiness? And thousands of miles away, I, too, am the victim of their rules."

Noel: "You sound pretty angry to me, Becky." (Becky silently stares at the floor). (Pause) Noel turns to David: "What is going through you as you listen to Becky right now, David?"

David: "I don't know what to say. I have been honest with her from the beginning. But I still feel it's my fault. I should have walked away from the relationship with Becky when I had the chance. I wasn't strong enough. I am causing pain for her, myself, and maybe even my relatives."

Becky: "Don't get too dramatic, David. We both know I didn't make it easy for you to run away." (All three attempt a smile.)

The session continues with Noel asking David how he views the tradition of his village. David answers that he respects the tradition, that he is not convinced its time has come and gone. He sees more harmony there than in other societies he has visited. His frustration is not so much with his tradition but with his fate. He cannot accept that this unhappiness is thrown upon him. He did not want to fall in love. He was content before. David has always believed strongly in fate and destiny, that he cannot keep major events from happening. On the other hand, he is an educated person who takes responsibility for his own actions. Thus there is a tension within his worldview regarding this situation. He feels guilty but also rebels against fate.

FRAME OF REFERENCE AND WORLDVIEW

In the last chapter we discussed frame of reference to explain the cognitive, experiential, and value gaps between persons involved in intercultural dialogue. We see the significance of frame of reference very clearly in the encounter between Noel, Becky, and David. Noel and

Becky are likely to agree that David should be free to marry the woman
he loves. To a certain degree, David might agree with that, but there is
another, much more deeply rooted part of him that reminds him of his
allegiance to the community. It appears Noel has no way of crossing
over in interpathy to the worldview that so informs David's thoughts,
emotions, and behavior. Noel looks at the world differently when it
comes to marriage. The individual is more important than the filial
community. We are reminded of our discussion about codes in the previous chapter, as well as the distinction between egocentric and holistic
cultures. David is in fact stuck between his own, traditional worldview
and Becky's and Noel's.

In one of two propositions Derald Sue claims that cross-cultural
counseling effectiveness is most likely to be enhanced when the counselor and the client share the same worldview (Sue 1981, 104). In a
second proposition he states that "cross-cultural counseling effectiveness is most likely to be enhanced when the counselor uses counseling
modalities and defines goals consistent with the life experiences/
cultural experiences of the client (Sue 1981, 106/107). The first
proposition deals with worldview, the second with what I have called
"frame of reference." I will first discuss the latter.

As has been made clear through our previous discussion, we need
awareness and skills to set the stage for cross-cultural pastoral care. But
in addition we need a meeting point, something that provides common
ground in the pastoral context, something that reflects the life of both
caregiver and care seeker, however small and irrelevant at first glance.

If caregiver and care seeker succeed in finding a common ground of
values, knowledge, and experience from which to start their exploration
together, that common ground could also be an important safeguard
against imposing the caregiver's value judgments. The more care seeker
and caregiver have common understandings at their disposal, the more
likely they are to come to a common interpretation of the care seeker's
problems.

Since persons and their cultures are in process, so to a great extent
are the frames of reference they use to communicate, for frame of reference reflects meaning-providing processes. There is power in Noel's
frame of reference, since it can influence how David and Becky see
themselves, their community, and their value system. Thus, if Noel's
frame of reference is largely in harmony with David's, he can affirm

David's self-concept, his feelings about his family, and his worldview. On the other hand, if there is incongruence between David and Noel's overall frame of reference, Noel's convictions could become threatening in all three of those areas. Noel's frame of reference is largely in harmony with Becky's with respect to marriage, and as such Becky's concept of herself as someone who is not wrong to love David and her value system are affirmed. On the other hand, David's frame of reference and Noel's frame of reference largely conflict, and Noel may to a certain degree be threatening David's self-concept, view of his community, and value system. Although Noel may be aware of this dissonance and is ready to approach David with cross-cultural skills, a battle is imminent between Noel's visceral reaction to arranged marriages and the understanding Noel knows he has to show David to be a good pastor. But Noel's awareness and skills are largely cognitive and superficial. The underlying friction between Noel's view of marriage and his pastoral sensitivity remains. Thus the potential exists for what is often called "cognitive dissonance" between David and Noel.

If Noel poses specific challenges to David out of his own frame of reference, the intercultural encounter influences many facets of David's complex experience. S.R. Strong argues that counseling "may be conceptualized as an interpersonal influence process in which the counselor uses his social power to influence the client's attitude and behavior (Strong 1969, 215–24). Noel can be as client-centered in his counseling style as possible, but it is likely that he will consciously or semiconsciously attempt to influence David in one way or another by the way he asks his questions or by the feelings he emphasizes when exhibiting empathy or simply communicating nonverbally. The research done by Jack Bilmes and Stephen Boggs illustrates this. When observing a group of participants discussing the meaning a shared experience had for them personally, they found that the understanding of the situation itself was constantly open to negotiation and reinterpretation as the participants redefined the issues. The people in the group acted as if meanings were already determined previously by each of them, when in fact these meanings largely came about in the group process (Marsella, Sharp, Ciborowski 1979, 69/70).

If meanings are negotiable in general social encounters, it would seem that a person such as David who seeks help and makes himself vulnerable to criticism from his caregiver would also be willing to compromise the meaning he is experiencing.

It is apparent that the pastor's attitudes and convictions with regard to the problems at hand in cross-cultural pastoral counseling are informed to a large extent by different processes of meaning than the attitudes and convictions of the parishioner. But there are possible dangers underlying the desire to influence.

First, there is danger of the influence being irrelevant. Second, there is danger of the influence taking place without the caregivers' understanding their own attitudes and convictions. Third, there is danger of losing sight of the total needs of the care receiver. Fourth, it is possible that the person seeking help will reject the influence and possibly the relationship with the caregiver. Fifth, there is a possibility the caregiver will fail to understand why the attitudes and convictions of the other are so different, thereby prompting a strong emotional reaction by the care seeker. Finally, there is a danger that caregivers are not capable of influencing the care seekers in the way the caregivers see fit.

When making changes, people need nonthreatening frames of reference they can accept so they can prevent discontinuity and instability. Therefore the caregiver should operate from a frame of reference that does not significantly contradict the frame of reference of the care seeker, thereby narrowing the gap between empathy and interpathy. Let us try to examine these questions more deeply with respect to David, Becky and Noel.

First, what influence does Noel want to carry into David's and Becky's life? He would like to tell David and Becky that there is a way for them to be happy together without severing David's bonds with his clan.

Second, on what basis does he try to tell them this? He does so on the basis of the emotions and thinking process he has discerned in the couple's verbal and nonverbal communication with the aid of the cross-cultural pastoral care and counseling skills and awareness. Inevitably his discernment is subjective, for he filters the couple's communication and pain through his own experience. Intuitively he will be searching for parallels and analogies within his own life, but his efforts are likely to remain tentative with regard to David. He may be able to formulate an analogy for himself, but he may not be able to formulate it in terms David can comprehend. Noel needs ideas and symbols that can convey to David the meaning he is grasping or coming close to grasping. These must be ideas and symbols that David and he profess to share, so that confusion or conflict may be avoided.

This simultaneously approximates an answer to a third question about the form Noel will use to get his message across. Whether he seeks to speak to David through short, interpathic sentences, through a story, or by referring to a movie scene he remembers, Noel must convey the meaning he considers precious in ideas and symbols David understands. This requires that David comprehend those ideals and symbols.

There are many lines of communication through which influence reaches people, who in turn find themselves at the ever-moving intersection of those lines. At a certain decisive moment or series of moments, the lines that bear in on David's life will touch or intersect the lines that shape or have shaped Noel's life. Noel's task is to facilitate the birth of these moments.

It may not be possible to eradicate the impact the caregiver has on the worldview of the care seeker. But obviously we would want to come as close as possible to guaranteeing that our impact is beneficial, both for the moment and in the long run. If we wish to make an effort to guarantee this, it is essential that the different perspectives the pastor shares with the care seeker do not threaten the self-concept and values of the care seeker in the broadest understanding of these terms. To avoid such a threat, a shared frame of reference should be sought. This could be a story or a line from a song or hymn, something that expresses what they both believe and accept, echoes from inside their worldviews, and provides a meeting point or stability as they both continue to change. Noel could engage in a dialogue with David about the meaning of marriage according to stories from both the Old and New Testaments. The Bible represents a part of their frame of reference they share as Christians. This does not mean forcing David into accepting Noel's position; instead, it means opening the door to mutual understanding. This can prevent the worldview informing David's frame of reference from being affected adversely, and a threat to cultural codes is thus avoided.

Both frame of reference and worldview have been repeatedly mentioned, but what is the relationship between the two? At first glance they may both appear to be cognitive in nature, but from a wholistic perspective, cognitive processes are not divorced from emotions or behavior. Worldview entails the way people judge the world around them, including what is beautiful or despicable, what is moral and wrong, what is wise and foolish, what our rights, as well as our responsibilities, are. The list goes on. But worldview also determines how people view themselves and the community of which they are a part. Conversely the family, community, and society in which we belong to a large extent determine our worldview.

Family, community, and society also help determine frame of reference. Frame of reference is the reservoir containing the information, values, experiences, knowledge, and tradition we utilize to fashion and refashion our worldview. In that process we make logical sense of the information, values, experiences, knowledge and tradition. People's worldviews may differ, but if their frames of reference overlaps at certain points, a common ground may be discovered.

ELEMENTS OF WORLDVIEW

In more detail, what is encompassed under worldview? Is it just a general philosophy of life? Again, I take a wholistic view. Worldview is a set of beliefs, values, or convictions in process essential to one's perception of one's environment, as well as of oneself and God. It is important to realize that the perception of environment, self, and God are interrelated. To a great extent David's environment is responsible for his self-concept. The people around him taught him that he was good if he obeyed certain rules and followed certain traditions, and not so good if he did not. His worth as a human being was judged against the background of society's expectations. These expectations told him whether it was good to be a vocal child or more appropriate to be a quiet youngster. They told him how old he should be before he marries and how much money he should send home to his family. Those expectations also taught him that he was to marry the woman selected for him. The community also taught him to believe a certain way, to speak to God a certain way, and to have a certain perception of how God looks on humans who do not obey the decrees of their elders. But when David moved away from his village, his cultural experience was supplemented, and so his worldview, although an essential part of his culture, evolved, as well. However, the cultural forces impacting his life could not always evolve and exist in harmony. Clashes and friction were inevitable. And at this moment of encounter, these three very different persons, an Asian male, a European American female, and their African American pastor, are briefly thrown together at a crucial juncture in David's life, as well as Becky's. The clash of meaning providing processes has reached a crisis point. They are riddled with guilt, plagued by fear, and jolted by anger. The forces of cultures that so enrich their lives at times now threaten to create irreparable damage. Worldviews rub against each other like crusts of land riding on restless continental plates. Everything is affected, the way they see the other, themselves, the people who raised them, the God they believe brought them together so irresistibly. David no longer knows which voices he should listen to, for they compete for influence in his worldview.

It is in the jumble of worldview elements that powerful emotions drift to the surface. David may be allowed to call into question the traditions of his ancestors, but for Becky or Noel to do so is quite another matter. Everything David is or has been or believes he should be is being called into question. As they speak, he is reevaluating himself, the family, the community, the society to which he belongs, and the philosophical tenets that undergird his existence. He is caught in a tragedy of his own making, which nevertheless he believes came about largely beyond his control.

Some clarification is needed about the relationship of faith, religion, and worldview. Earlier the point was made that religion is part of culture—the part of culture expressed in beliefs, norms, values, rituals, and so forth—that represents a response to the divine or the supernatural. It mostly comes to expression in the community and is generally observable. It informs frame of reference and consequently has a large part in shaping worldview. Faith is really a more emotional and spiritual dimension of worldview. Worldview, in the rational form of personal theology, makes sense of faith in the realm of the everyday. Religion can be conducive to the growth of faith, but it may also obstruct it.

THE PASTORAL TASK

If Noel wants to show interpathy to David, he must find a way to bridge the worldview chasm existing between himself and David with respect to love and marriage. Their respective worldviews are not likely to change, although in honest dialogue they may reach a mutual understanding.

Nevertheless, the cross-cultural pastoral care context is not the ideal setting for spirited dialogue, because the vulnerable care seeker has an emotional disadvantage in the conversation. It is not the time to search for worldview dissimilarities, just as it is also not the time to whitewash them. David, Noel, and Becky need a place to meet, a common ground, a bridge over the chasm. For this they need to turn to their frame of reference, their vast reservoir of experiences, information, and knowledge, to find elements they have in common; perhaps a book they all love or a movie they once saw or a Bible passage they have read, even if half forgotten. I remember hearing one of the great Islamic leaders in Indonesia who had been trained in the Middle East being interviewed on television on the subject of Hollywood movies he loved. Cultural pluralism divides people, for the days are over that we have almost everything in common. At the same time, the days are also past when people of the world have almost nothing in common.

Noel, David, and Becky have much in common. David has spent many years in North America already, and the experiences and knowledge gained are part of his frame of reference. However, the subject at hand will point to very few direct parallels in North American life. The best meeting place, the best shared element of their frames of reference are biblical stories. Has Ruth perhaps something to say about marriage and estrangement? Do Jacob's trials in marriage open the door to new perspectives? Is David, like Abraham, called to a new land, or like Moses, called back to the land of his origins? These stories do not provide formulas for problem solving, but they do provide common ground, and in the case of biblical stories, sacred ground, to stand on together and become better acquainted.

It will not be possible to know the background of every cultural group, and that may not be necessary. The person seeking help can help guide the caregiver. But it is important for the cross-cultural caregiver to be well read and open to new information. Counseling models and psychology books are not sufficient to broaden a frame of reference. But a healthy interest in the way people think and feel and act in other places, as well as an antennae for popular cultures, are prerequisites. Also helpful is the ability to discern the story aspect in human lives and to see how it is analogous to the story aspect of other people. We will discuss this further in another chapter.

Worldview is one of the three diagnostic categories in cross-cultural pastoral care and counseling. The problem should be examined as far as possible in the light of the care seeker's values. Some basic information concerning faith and other worldview background should be provided. The caregiver can ask the care seeker which religious ideas or ethical principles most speak or spoke to them, particularly with regard to the problem at hand. And the care seeker can ask which religious stories have most touched the care seeker.

Caregivers could give an example of a story they personally might find meaningful if they were confronting the care seeker's difficulties. This helps the analogical process in the care seeker's mind. However, the search for worldview should at no time be divorced from the discussion of the presenting problem and the larger context in which it functions.

In spite of the fact that this framework demands alertness on the part of the caregiver, the emphasis should remain on listening and responding briefly so that the caregiver might start detecting dissonance between conflicting aspects of worldviews. The caregiver should further try to ascertain the general spiritual condition of the person seeking help: Is there a sense of divine providence? of gratitude? Does doubt have a crippling effect? Is the person besieged by anger or guilt toward God? Does existential anxiety occur frequently?

As light is shed on worldview and the other two diagnostic categories, a picture will start to emerge of the conflicts, tensions, dissonance, and incongruence that tear at the heartstrings of the person seeking help, that drive him or her toward increasing brokenness and away from wholeness.

ETHICS

Ara is an Armenian American male in his late fifties and a successful citrus grower. He is an intelligent and hard-working man who embodies the "American dream." A poor immigrant from a strife-torn region of the world, he has succeeded in bringing the fruits of his labor to his family.

But Ara is bitter. He is bitter because of the changes he sees going on around him and in his life. After the death of his wife, he has grown lonely and has involved himself in church work to fill the emptiness. But while he was serving on a church committee, occasional heated dialogues in area churches flared up about labor disputes, conservation of water, and the use of pesticides. It was bad enough that there were people accusing the growers of treating farm laborers unfairly. It was bad enough that the state was debating water rights in his valley and that environmentalists were accusing his friends of harming farmworkers by using pesticides. But that these issues were discussed in church and that church people pointed the finger at hard-working pioneers like Ara—that was too much. He felt he had done everything right and was being accused of doing everything wrong.

To make matters worse, one of his daughters, Elaine, had become an activist on environmental issues. He had learned a lot from her, but had also been deeply hurt by her fiery accusations that he had been indifferent, that he was "too concerned about the money." Who was he making that money for?

On one occasion he complained to Gary Fernandez, one of his pastors, about what was happening:

"You know, pastor, I feel old. I have worked and worked all my life to give my children what Armenians haven't had for generations, a good life full of opportunities. And now it seems I do everything wrong."

Gary: "What do you mean, 'Do everything wrong'? I think you are a fine man who does a lot for the church."

Ara: "Well, you know Elaine is always criticizing us growers for their attitude toward the farmworkers and everything else." Well, . . . (his eyes go misty).

Gary: "Sounds like you feel she's hurting you, Ara."

Ara: "No, I wouldn't call it hurting. Well, yes, maybe. It's just that I wish my wife . . . (Gary hands him a tissue, and Ara blows his nose. Gary holds Ara's hand) (pause) I wish she was here."

Gary: "I know you do, Ara, I know you do. She was a very supportive person."

Ara: "I'm tired of feeling like I'm bad, because I don't believe I am. Can't you talk to Elaine. I have tried to make her see things my way, but she just doesn't agree."

Gary: "I'm afraid there's not much I can do for you. It's between you and your daughter. But I am concerned about your relationship with her, and maybe we could talk all together once."

Ara: "No, it's not that we don't get along. It's just that I thought you could talk some sense into her. She listens to you, and you don't seem to be such a fanatic about these issues."

Gary is placed in a very difficult situation. He is a gentle and friendly man who always seems able to see life through the eyes of his parishioners. He can always look at an issue from a number of angles. This has made him an effective and much-loved pastor. He thinks it is his responsibility to give guidance through caring, not through confrontation. But Gary, as a Latino American, feels strongly about the rights of farm workers and about the environment. He has been trying to get the congregation involved in outreach to poor farm workers and has gotten to know many of the workers and the staggering problems they face. On the other hand, he cannot hurt a grieving widower like Ara, who treasures so many tales of tragedy of his Middle Eastern forebears.

To Gary, Ara's problem raises both pastoral and ethical questions. For Ara, it not so much a question of ethics as it is a matter of feeling betrayed. In cross-cultural pastoral care, this situation is quite common. The caregiver sees clear wrongdoing, while the care seeker's worldview does not sensitize him or her to that particular issue. This raises the question of *distortion* in cross-cultural pastoral care. On the one hand, we could say Gary has a real moral case. One could even use the books of the Old Testament as an illustration of the need for social justice. Thus there is the possibility of Gary's worldview distorting his interpretation of Ara' s situation. On the other hand, Ara's worldview may be distorting his view of other people and their claims

Ara's and Gary's worldviews overlap at many points, particularly where their Christian faith is concerned. But in other areas, their worldviews diverge. This is not just a cognitive issue (as was made clear when gender issues where alluded to in chapter 1), but involves Ara's self-concept and his sense of belonging among friends with the same profession. Gary cannot offer a model of the new person Ara should become at his advanced age. He must address distortion by patiently guiding Ara into an exploration of the incongruence between what he believes, how he sees himself, and where he belongs. Gary can be aided by the biblical frame of reference they share.

The following principle emerges: The caregiver should approach the total worldview of the care seeker with great care, attempting to operate from the care seeker's perspective while being conscious of distortion that enters communication.

4

CROSS-CULTURAL PERSONALITY AND IDENTITY

Bill, an experienced hospital chaplain in a large hospital, meets a middle-aged lawyer from Indonesia who is hospitalized for a broken leg and ankle from a fall on ice. The man, Musa, is in the United States for continuing education, pursuing a doctorate degree. He is an accomplished lawyer in the Indonesian capital, but was raised in a fishing town on the island of Sulawesi in Eastern Indonesia. When he was a young, his mother was killed by a group of religious extremists who rampaged through the mountain village where his father was a lay pastor. Driven from their village, which was not far from the sea, the family settled at the edge of the predominantly Muslim fishing town, populated by the Bugis people, a cultural group known for their seafaring prowess. Musa, however, was a Toraja. The Toraja are not a sea, but a mountain people who are overwhelmingly Protestant.

When Musa was very small, his sister accidently cut his face with a knife, leaving a frightful scar and robbing him of his eyesight in one eye. He remembers being teased continuously by the children in the neighborhood, which seems to have had a significant influence on how he sees himself.

Bill, a European American, who had mostly been quiet as he listened in fascination to Musa's story asked:

"How did that make you feel?"

Musa: "Oh, I don't know how much I thought about it, but I always thought my handicap gave me an excuse . . ."

Bill: "An excuse for what."

Musa: "For not doing quite as well in school."

Bill: "Why was that?"

Musa: "Because I had only one good eye, so I really only had to do half as well."

Bill: "Mmmm, that's interesting. But how do you explain being so successful now? I am sure you have surpassed all those children who called you names."

Musa: "Well yes, but there is still more to reach."

Bill: "What is it you want to reach exactly?"

Musa: "I'm not quite sure, but I am not yet at peace."

As they continue their conversation, Musa's preoccupation with advancing himself reveals that he has not quite forgotten the voices of those children, that he is still listening to tapes telling him he does not measure up. Musa eloquently proceeds with his story of high school and college experiences in places all over Indonesia and his studies in Australia. He mentions that his wife is from a cultural group on the island of Java, and that the Javanese ways are quite different from the traditions of his own people. He met her when he was studying in Java at one of the prestigious universities. He talks about how poor they were when they married, that he even had to borrow bus fare to go ask for his wife's hand. There is pride in his eyes as Musa pulls himself up in his bed in an attempt to get comfortable. Later the conversation shifts to the prognosis for his recovery, before Bill has to leave.

A CROSS-CULTURAL UNDERSTANDING OF PEOPLE

Musa's self-understanding is an important part of his problem. He wants to prove himself to others, not to specific people in his life, but really to the audience of people whose voices he has internalized. This raises the question of self concept, the second of the diagnostic categories. Before we discuss how persons in cross-cultural pastoral care see themselves, it is relevant to explore how caregivers should view people and personality in a cross-cultural setting.

We continue to operate with a definition of culture as process. Cultures, that is, meaning providing processes, are constantly being shaped and reshaped. They influence and are influenced by the changing social context in which caregiver and care seeker live, and by the philosophy of life adhered to by those they interact with in that changing social context. Musa's meaning providing processes changed as he settled into his life in central Java after growing up in southern Sulawesi. He was exposed not only to the Javanese world, but also to the world of students who thought and acted differently from the secondary school students in his home region. To a certain extent, his way of viewing the world changed, for he took new meaning providing processes into himself. Similar things can be said about his experiences in Australia and the United States. Thus Musa has become a new person with new perceptions and perspectives, and he has been influenced by new environments and new ideas. But not only has he been influenced; he has influenced and continues to influence others. He will return from the United States with a worldview that is part Sulawesi, part Javan, part Australian, part American, merged in a flowing river of unique experiences. With this mixture of experience, Musa will react to and view his surroundings in Jakarta, thereby bringing new meaning providing processes to those who have not yet experienced them.

Human beings refashion themselves as they continuously filter old and new cultural influences. Musa is not powerless to choose which meaning providing processes will become part of his developing person, but his power is reduced as he opens himself up, not only cognitively but also emotionally to the subtle authority of a helping professional such as Bill.

Several issues regarding understanding people in a cross-cultural setting are important. First, the person is changing continually. Second, peoples' surroundings, particularly their relationships, are constantly changing as they meet new people and as the people they are used to relating to are themselves changing. Third, peoples' manner of interpreting experience changes. This means that three important processes are going on continuously: the self is changing, relationships are changing, and ways of seeing the world are changing.

The self cannot become what it is without the input of the surrounding world. Most personality theorists agree that the environment helps form personality.

When viewing themselves, individuals are largely dependent on the views persons in their environment have provided them with. Michelle Rosaldo claims that "culture . . . is . . . the very stuff of which our subjectivities are created (Shweder and LeVine 1984, 150), a view echoed and complemented by Richard Shweder and Edmund Bourne, who stress that "it is sobering to acknowledge that our sense of personal inviolatability is a violatable social gift, the product of what *others* are willing to respect and protect us from, the product of the way we are handled and reacted to, the products of the rights and privileges we are granted by others in numerous 'territories of the self' " Shweder and LeVine 1984, 194).

Additionally, the way we see the world is a determining factor in how we view ourselves, for the kind of world we see influences our role in perpetuating or changing it.

It is interesting to apply these different spheres of self, surroundings/relationships, and worldview to decision making, which is an important phase in pastoral care and counseling. There is reason to believe that in the process of gaining new perspective and achieving change, a person considers the group, as well as normative beliefs. Four components determine the intention to perform an act: first, the emotional implications of the act; second, beliefs about performing the act and the evaluation of those consequences; third, the perceived appropriateness of the act for the subject's reference group (norms) and people holding similar positions in the social structure (roles); finally, personal normative beliefs with regard to the behavior of interest (Marsella, Sharp, Ciborowski 1979, 152/153).

A holistic model of personality has been developed by Francis Hsu. This model is broader than most theories of personality in which the environment has a more prominent place. It proposes that personality consists of seven spheres: the unconscious, the subconscious in the Freudian sense, the unexpressed conscious, the expressed conscious, intimate society, the sphere of useful relationships, and the sphere of distant relationships. The outside world is found beyond these spheres (Hsu 1971).

No model of personality can be conclusive in its applicability to cross-cultural pastoral care and counseling, but the majority of theories accept that environment and worldview, especially religious worldview, play a significant part. Because three aspects of self, relationship/environment, and worldview function as dynamic and related processes informed by meaning providing processes, it is important that consideration of these aspects form an integral part of our methodology in cross-cultural pastoral care and counseling. For as has been stressed, theories of personality do underlie counseling methodologies.

Worldview has already been explored. The relationship/environment aspect is the focus of the next chapter. Below we will further examine the aspect of self. The discussion will home in on identity, the person's self-concept.

UNDERSTANDING IDENTITY

I again propose that identity be seen in a holistic light. By this I mean that the concept of identity should not be divided up in "sub-identities."

Musa formed his identity by evaluating the teasing remarks of his "friends" in the light of his already not-so-positive self-image as a refugee from Toraja land. That helped shape his identity or at least part of it. There are cultural, psycho-social, and other aspects to that identity, but their differentiation might reduce instead of explain the person that Musa is.

It is generally believed that identity development is completed by the end of adolescence, but it is probably clearer to say that core identity is completed by then, because our self-concept can change significantly over time, as the "racial/cultural identity development model" appears to confirm. It identifies stages of identity development in, among others, African Americans (Akinson, Morten, and Sue 1989). The first stage is the conformity stage, during which people are generally self-depreciating with regards to self and group, discriminatory toward other minority groups, and positive toward the dominant group. In the second, dissonance stage, in each of these areas there is a conflict between an appreciating and a depreciating attitude. In the resistance and immersion stage, the attitude toward self and group is positive and the attitude toward the dominant group is negative. In addition, the person struggles to decide whether to appreciate other minority groups or not. In the fourth introspection stage, the person retains a positive view of the group but also wishes to take distance and assert individuality. In the final integrative awareness stage, the person can appreciate self and all groups, although the person selectively appreciates certain subgroups of the dominant cultural group. As persons continue to be in process in dialogue with cultural processes, they change. In the previous chapter David rethinks his self-concept as he evaluates his predicament. Musa's self-concept is subject to change as he moves from culture to culture. While his core image of himself stays intact, he incorporates new ways of viewing himself. In fact, we can see Musa's identity as a handicapped, one-eyed child do battle with his identity as an accomplished professional, thus causing him to experience identity confusion. We find Musa struggling with the legacy of the past. It appears he cannot shake the image he had of himself as a child. All the successive positive experiences have not been able to transform that image, and the need to prove himself continues to preoccupy him.

Musa's identity seems to have been formed mostly at a young age, but then his identity is clearly evolving through the exposure to other cultures and in his marriage. Still his renewed identity does not succeed in erasing the old one, which, ironically, is largely determined by Musa's interaction with his cultural groups. So in his current identity, Musa is really at odds with the preadolescent identity that has become thoroughly rooted. Musa is in process, and in that process Bill may be able to help him.

In the formation of identity, identification with others has an important role. It is because of identification with significant people that human beings form and reform their self-concept. Thus the people we identify with are given great power to determine our image of self. During childhood and adolescence we are more vulnerable to being shaped through identifications, specifically with parents. Musa identified with the handicapped image and so far has not been able to shake it. But there were other offsetting identifications, such as with his father, who served as a lay preacher, an identification that contributed to his growth toward successful and functional adulthood.

In cross-cultural pastoral care and counseling, it is imperative to see that self-concept in relationship to worldview defines a person's role in the community and society as a whole.

THE PASTORAL TASK

If there is an opportunity for Bill and Musa to meet again, the central focus should probably be the question of why Musa feels the insatiable desire to prove himself. Where are the roots of his restlessness? Is the restlessness due mostly to his basic personality structure, or to his experiences as a child? How can his self-concept evolve so that he does not cause himself unnecessary suffering? Bill could use some cognitive tech-

niques to put Musa's fears of insignificance in perspective, but he faces
the problem of differing worldviews. As much time as Musa may have
spent in countries with predominantly egocentric cultures emphasizing
the power of the individual to succeed, the voices of a painful childhood
take forever to forget. One of the essential challenges is to help Musa
stop playing the tapes of the past, without calling into question the le-
gitimacy of the world that molded him.

WORLDVIEW, IDENTITY, AND SENSE OF BELONGING

The "internal and external control and responsibility" model (Rotter
1966) provides insight into the differences between persons who look
at themselves as being in control of their situation and those who see
themselves as powerless to control their life situation. The model also
distinguishes between those who view themselves as responsible for
their situation and those who tend to emphasize the responsibility of
others. Each person consciously or unconsciously operates with a
worldview about *control* and *responsibility*. Therefore there are four different categories of people. First, those with an internal locus of control
and an internal locus of responsibility believe they are both in control
and responsible for most of their situations. Second, people with an external locus of control and an external locus of responsibility tend to be
rather passive. Third, some people have an internal locus of control and
an external locus of responsibility. Finally, other people have an external
locus of control and an internal locus of responsibility. With regard to
his handicap, Musa might blame his sister. For his family's suffering, he
might blame those who killed his mother, while at the same time seeing
his misery as God's will. Overall he feels he has control and responsibility, so interestingly he has acquired an individualistic way of viewing
his place in the world. Again we must be reminded that people are in
process and in a pluralistic context seldom fit into one category. They
may even operate with different categories in different situations.

Identity is tied to individuals' sense of belonging to particular groups
of people with whom they feel an affinity. People may identify with several groups with different values. Because they are emotionally affected
by these groups, they must be affected by group members' worldview
also. The values of the group become part of their frame of reference,
because values are inseparable from the group that holds those values.

Caregivers, when challenging the worldview of care seekers, can threaten care seekers' identity and sense of belonging. The result of this could be a grief or crisis reaction because the care seeker is vulnerable to begin with. In contrast, when caregiving is only minimally inter-cultural, that is, when the participants share the basic cultural backgrounds, an automatic sensitivity to the other's worldview can be expected. Caregiver and care seeker have been exposed to comparable values that are continuously reinforced in a shared environment. Topics will be easily chosen and interpreted by analogy.

When an individual's worldview is challenged, the world that nurtured the worldview, as well as the individual's role in that world is also called into question.

Human beings are to a certain extent in the process of developing a sense of belonging in one community and then another, whether the community is family or church or a group of colleagues. Musa, a devout Christian and who experiences a strong sense of belonging in the church, will register a strong emotional reaction when the church is vehemently criticized. Yet he belongs also to the Toraja people, although he does not feel an overwhelming affinity with that group. Thus criticism of the Toraja is not likely to upset him greatly.

Knowing that identity does not develop on its own, we could say that identity is a plant that can flourish only in the soil of belonging. The idea of being able to "find oneself" by separating from the belonging group may be popular in contemporary North American society, but it may be largely a fallacy. How can we know who we are if we do not belong anywhere?

Identity and sense of belonging are really two sides of one coin. Identity is the personal side, and sense of belonging, the collective side. Identification is necessary for either to come about.

When counseling, we must, of course, begin with the presenting problem, for anyone would want a caregiver to take his or her problem seriously. The person should be encouraged to tell this story completely without becoming repetitious or overly detailed. Of utmost importance are the caregiver's appropriate attending and basic responding skills, as well as his or her awareness of cultural codes, the care seeker's expectations of the caregiver, and the control/responsibility worldview.

As caregivers listen and respond succinctly, they form a picture of the care seeker's self-concept-in-process. Is the person's self-image of someone who is weak, stubborn, bright, attractive, jealous, or clumsy? Once the problem has been sketched between the lines of the care seeker's unique story, ideally the sojourn of the person as it relates to the presenting problem should be summarized. Musa's difficulty essentially lies in an identity problem of diffusion caused by a conflict between the self-image of his childhood and his current self-concept (see chapter 6).

To assist in the process of determining problems in relation to identity, caregivers should organize their questions and reflection as far as possible around the theme of identification. For instance, who were the significant people the care seeker identified with as he or she was growing up? Which identifications are prominent now? What were or are those people like? Was the person ever hurt by the person with whom he or she identified? Should these identifications continue? To lighten up the conversation, some questions about favorite movies, books, stories could be asked.

The caregiver should attempt to extract information that could connect the identifications to the person's sense of identity, and both of these to the problem. Another important question concerns the identifications conducive to the growth of the problem and those that might help eliminate it.

Our discussion leads us to the next principle, namely that the caregiver shall operate with an understanding that identity is always in process and that it is related to worldview and sense of belonging. At one point, the self-concept of the care seeker should be addressed, either directly or indirectly, without losing touch of the presenting problem.

5

ASSESSING SENSE OF BELONGING

A young Native American woman named Judy approaches Marisa Phillips, her new pastor on a reservation in the intermountain west. Marisa, who is of Puerto Rican and European descent, was assigned to the reservation because of her cross-cultural experience. She has only met Judy a few times but knows Judy's mother, a member of the small congregation, quite well. It is late at night and Judy asks to come in, without explaining what she is there for. Judy, a sometime hospital clerk who usually looks very well-groomed, appears unkempt and confused. She tells the pastor she has not been at home for four days. She has been drinking with her husband and some of their friends during that time. Judy had publicly expressed her good intentions not to drink anymore, but she explains that the life on the reservation depresses her to the point where she cannot face the day alone. Also she is afraid her husband will have an affair with one of the single women in their small group of drinking friends if she does not keep an eye on him.

Judy is really quite popular and a good worker, but the jobs she has held never seem to last. Except for a few people who work as ranch hands, nurses, or teachers, no one on the reservation seems to be permanently employed. So for Judy, drinking and watching television appear to be the only ways to escape the reservation without actually leaving it.

Judy's face hides all emotion. Marisa cannot quite decide whether she is not feeling anything or whether she is feeling too much to show any emotion. Being an extraverted person herself, Marisa finds it difficult to understand. Judy talks about her pain in short cryptic sentences and smiles faintly and shyly after each, as if she were trying to communicate that her suffering is either trivial or amusing and embarrassing. But as Marisa encourages Judy to tell her story, the subject of Judy's marriages comes up. She tells how her first husband, Joe, a European American, a truckdriver, and the father of her oldest daughter, was fatally wounded in a car accident in a large city. Judy was living in a town a few hundred miles from the reservation where she was going to college. She explains that her present husband, Billy, who is much older than Judy, is jealous of Joe, as well as of other men. The extent of her suffering slowly becomes obvious to Marisa as Judy grows sullen. But in the process of counseling Judy, it occurs to Marisa that Judy's problem goes beyond drinking, her grief over Joe, and her anger at Billy. An existential problem looms large in the background. Judy is lost, lost between worlds, feeling caught between a melancholic longing for the rootless life outside the isolated reservation and the desire for the predictability of her home, although that is inevitably accompanied by inertia and boredom. When she feels all resistance to despair slipping away, she wants to drink, but afterwards she feels that her sense of dignity and control has faded as her life appears even more dismal. Marisa asks at one point:

"Judy, do you like it here? I mean, do you want to be here?"

Judy: "Some days I do. Some days I love the sky and the mesas in the distance and my Dad's grouchy face and the coyotes howling in the distance. I know my grandparents are buried here. That's something. Other days I could hang myself from the belltower. That would get their attention."

Marisa: "Whose attention, Judy?"

Judy: "I don't know. My pig of a husband maybe, or my knucklehead parents, or the governor (smiles)."

Marisa: "Or mine."

Judy: "Yeah, you'll do. After all, you own the belltower."

Marisa: "What about Joe. Do you want Joe to notice?"

Judy: "Now don't get weird on me; Joe's history."

Marisa: "Is he?"

Judy: (silence) "I suppose not." (The bottom part of her face shows the beginning of a smile).

ALIENATION AND SENSE OF BELONGING

Judy is caught between the life in the "white" world and her life on the reservation, although neither life is overly tempting. She calls herself an "Indian," but she is nostalgic for her experiences in Joe's world, too. While Judy's presenting problems are her alcoholism, her grief for Joe, and her relationship with Billy, the extra complicating factor is her sense of alienation.

In Judy's case, we can see that she is not only lost between her memories of the European American world she used to inhabit and her ties to her ancestral land, but she also goes back and forth between the church and a particular group of friends who encourage her alcoholic behavior. Judy is not making a gradual transition from identification with one belonging group to identification with another, for there is neither gradual movement from one group to another nor a harmony between her identification with the two belonging groups. Her ambivalence makes her growth impossible. Part of the reason for this is that the reservation does not offer many alternatives. The sky is endless there, but life is depressingly limited.

Clearly she feels an affinity with both the larger societies of the reservation and of the predominantly European American world as close as two hundred miles away. But she had also at one point found a place among smaller groups, including Joe's drug addicted friends, and her compatriots on the reservation. But when disgust brought her to the church door every few years, the very small church community would be her home for three months or so as she took part in every potluck supper and study group the weary parish leadership was able to put together.

As discussed in the previous chapter, identification is key in the exploration of sense of belonging. Judy is most likely to identify intensely with the groups to which she most feels she belongs. The pastor therefore encourages Judy to share information about the groups that make her feel most at home. These will also be the groups that contribute significantly to her self-concept-in-process. She is likely to feel pressure to conform her behavior to the behavior of her primary belonging group, so as not to damage her self-concept, which is always subject to change. For instance, when Judy feels alienated from her group of friends on the reservation and moves toward active participation in the life of the local church community, she conforms her behavior to the behavior of the church group. This does not mean she is not genuine or that she is showing contradictory personality traits, but merely that she is torn between different belonging groups and ways of viewing herself.

If Judy identifies with her friends on the reservation, if it is their behavior to which she seeks to conform, then they represent an important belonging group. That belonging group will help determine how she views her decisions about life, and their values will influence her behavior. Identification with a negative group will destroy her sense of identity. These negative identifications are often set in motion because of a sense of belonging to groups that do not have the well-being of the person in mind, but that instead use people for their own purposes. On the other hand, if she identifies with her pastor and her mother, who is active in the life of the congregation, and the other Native American Christians she has met at national conferences in the past, then the church is also a significant belonging group.

THE PASTORAL TASK

Marisa probes for information concerning Judy's sense of belonging (which I define as the experience and conviction of being a part of something larger) within communities by getting her to express her feelings about her family and friends on the reservation and about the friends she and Joe shared. With whom does she feel most comfortable? Who accepts her most? Where can she be herself? To whom can she go to talk about her grief?

The pastor then evaluates the connection between Judy's sense of belonging, her identity, her worldview, and her presenting problem. Marisa looks at all the factors hampering the alleviation of Judy's suffering. Judy's alienation is one of those factors. Her belonging to a group of people engaged in self-destructive behavior on a regular basis is another. Her lack of purpose is another. Her drinking yet another. Thus the connection between her grief, her drinking, her will to belong, and her alienation from her environment are all brought into sharp focus in the exchange between Judy and her pastor.

Marisa wants to affirm Judy's belonging within the Christian community and remind her subtly of the values of the church, without threatening

her sense of belonging in other groups. If Marisa's challenging Judy's destructive values leads to Judy's alienation from her other belonging
groups, the pastor will most likely do more damage than good. We must
remember that Judy's life is an amalgam. She cannot break with everything and start over in some other place. Her home is the reservation. Self-
imposed exile would mean denial of the larger story of her life and further
alienation. The primary culture and belonging group, in Judy's case the
Native Americans on the reservation, has been responsible for the development of most of her values. If the pastor pulls her away from those
values, it would mean threatening not only those values but also her sense
of belonging in the group that gave her those values. For instance, if the
pastor criticizes the return to ancient healing rituals as a way to bind the
wounds and regain a sense of identity, Judy could interpret Marisa's criticism as an attack on the people with whom Judy feels a strong connection.
And if the pastor criticizes her belonging group, Judy may hear negative
statements about herself, for Judy identifies with that group. So we can see
that value judgments are in essence inseparable from threats to sense of
belonging and identity.

Judy left the reservation to study, but she fell in love. The European
American man she loved reaffirmed the pattern of despair she had seen
growing on the reservation: substance abuse as a way to end the pain.
In her desire to belong outside the reservation, only he showed her the
way to go. No church community reached out to make her entry into a
new culture smooth. This shows that the task of the pastor goes beyond
counseling Judy to building a community vibrant enough for Judy to
belong to.

Concretely, there are several steps a caregiver could take to help
Judy. (1) Help her sort out her experiences outside the reservation, and
particularly help her move through and past her grief over the loss of
her first husband. (2) Help her face her alcoholism as the disease that it
is, and have her make a commitment to be treated and join an Alcohol-
ics Anonymous group sensitive to her cultural background (although
this may mean traveling a fair distance outside of the reservation). (3)
Help her realize that to be a part of the church and to care for her circle
of friends on the reservation are not necessarily mutually exclusive decisions, and that she can belong to other groups without having to dismiss these persons she cares about. (4) Help her see that to belong to
the church does not mean she has to become like her mother (who,

according to Judy, gossips too much), but that young people like her could help the church as a community become more dynamic. (5) This would mean that an important task facing the pastor would be to help make the congregation more attractive as a belonging group. The activities would have to be obvious, for instance in mid-week activities, special worship services, camping trips, and so forth. Also, the pastor would have to be seen as a person with whom the congregation could identify and be comfortable. This in turn would imply that the pastor would show willingness to step outside the attitudes stipulated by her own belonging groups and to try to understand how life is viewed by young Native Americans. (6) Through the pastor's sensitivity to Judy's belonging groups and her identification with individuals in those groups, Judy and Marisa could explore the behavior and values she has taken from those groups and people and evaluate them in terms of her present identity and her belonging in the Christian community.

THE WILL TO BELONG

Cross-cultural pastoral care raises the question of belonging, for if persons truly belong in a particular group or culture, why do they seek the help of someone outside that culture? They seek cross-cultural pastoral care because a representative of their primary culture group is not available. Or they seek help in a cross-cultural setting because they fear that a person from their cultural group may pass moral judgment on their actions or cannot be trusted to maintain confidentiality. People who seek help through cross-cultural pastoral care have to a certain degree "strayed from the flock" of their primary culture group, whether that is by choice or because they are forced to relate to a majority culture. As such, they are vulnerable. Judy is vulnerable. She grieves for the belonging group outside the reservation, and the pastor, as an outsider, is a representative of that culture to her.

Judy never lasted very long without belonging anywhere, as would be the case with most people. While in past decades theologians chose to focus on objectless anxiety as an existential condition, perhaps in these days of increasing mobility, readily available information, superficiality, and shallow commitments, the link between absence of belonging and chronic anxiety should become a main pastoral focus. While theologians and philosophers speak of the fear of nothingness, through our awareness of cross-cultural issues we can point to the threat of not belonging in an increasingly pluralistic world.

THE OTHER SIDE OF BELONGING

Belonging does not in itself guarantee positive experience. So often people seeking pastoral help have horrible memories of their belonging groups. They bring stories of abuse, humiliation, ridicule, or loneliness in the midst of those who were supposed to support them. They cannot wait to usher these memories into the distant recesses of their personal history. How many in pastoral work have not run up against the ghosts of the past in people's lives? What care seekers experienced as children still haunts them today. Childhood takes forever to forget if the experiences were very painful. There are many adults who, on a semiconscious level, are still trying to live up to the expectations of people in their past, some of whom may no longer be living; so many, like Musa, who are still trying to prove to their friends of days gone by that they are worthwhile. Somehow these people who influenced us during childhood continue to set some invisible standard by which we continue to measure ourselves. To a large extent these people still make up earlier belonging groups. Those old relationships often continue to be the ties that bind. We may run away from family or school friends, but their voices remain until they are dealt with. Most people want to feel they have a visible or invisible fan club of friends and relatives past and present whom they can count on to cheer them on as they make major decisions in life. If a person decides to become a pastor, he or she would like to think a certain number of people, living or dead, would respect him or her for having the dedication. If someone chooses social work or teaching, he or she wants people to approve of his or her sense of responsibility and willingness to care for the most vulnerable in society. If a person dreams of being successful in business, that person wants someone to tell him or her that being in business is wise if someone wishes to raise a family comfortably. Belonging groups are responsible for most of the "tapes" people play over and over for themselves.

All human beings are in transition from one belonging group to another. Those from a rural cultural background may go through that transition more slowly than others. Their group of closest friends and relatives may not change much over the years. Those who move from city to city, abroad and back home, in and out of a marriage are likely to feel more sharply the shock of having to shift belonging groups. Many of them may decide to belong nowhere and accept solitude and loneliness with relative contentment.

One of the tasks of the caregiver in cross-cultural pastoral care is to help persons to retain or gain a sense of belonging that nurtures their self-image and encourages a healthy worldview. Only seldom can the ties of the past be severed effortlessly.

READING BETWEEN THE LINES

When pastors try to help a person who, relatively speaking, shares their cultural background, the task of understanding is difficult enough already. But at least they can expect the other to comprehend expressions they propose as metaphors of the situation. There is a largely shared frame of reference: movies, songs, stories, places they have been can bring them together. They have more values in common. They know that what the other person's parents and teachers have tried to teach them is similar to what they themselves have received. They know what kind of humor to use to oil the relationship—whether to make fun of government officials, other authority figures, certain groups of people, or themselves. They can measure whether what they say will be harmless or harmful. Each person is a new book, but at least with some people they know how to read between the lines.

The concept of seeing persons as living texts is widely accepted among pastoral caregivers. With that understanding, cross-cultural pastoral care is not the setting for speed reading. The analysis is not complete without an understanding of where the text was written or is still being written. For this purpose, when addressing the question of self-image, we need to examine the larger story of a person's life. And at the heart of this larger story lies the question of belonging. However, if the caregiver approaches person and problem in a systematic way with the three diagnostic categories, including sense of belonging, the encounters do not necessarily have to be very lengthy.

Providing pastoral care across cultures continues to be a series of tenuous attempts at best, but sensitivity to the belonging issue can help dissolve the tension at the heart of cross-cultural pastoral care, namely discovering how to help without harming. Therefore in the process of a pastoral encounter, the caregiver needs to make a concerted effort to understand the level of belonging or affinity in relation to specific groups as a basis for helping people move naturally from one belonging group to another.

The crucial questions in the belonging category relate the person's sense of belonging to identification and the problem at hand. The questions include the following:

- At this time, what are the care seeker's primary cultural as well as identification groups? Do they include a group of students with a variety of religious backgrounds, the church, the family, or a combination of these?
- Does the caregiver detect that the care seeker has a significant sense of belonging in any of these groups. The family very often will be at the top the list.
- Is there any visible behavior attributable to a significant desire to belong and be accepted in any of these groups?
- Which groups seem to be influenced by the care seeker's presenting problem?
- Which groups, if any, carry responsibility for the problem?
- If possible, the caregiver should identify the groups with which identification or the will to belong is most powerful, as well as determine which groups have a direct interest in the problem.

The personal story has very little meaning when not placed in the context of the story of groups or persons. A failure to refer to these groups would mean the caregiver could not begin to comprehend the person in cross-cultural pastoral care. To a large extent the self-concept of individuals has been shaped by the people and conditions in their surroundings, but their self-concepts continue to be sanded and carved in interaction with the environment as they travel through the stages of life.

We have arrived at the following principle: The caregiver engaged in cross-cultural pastoral care must take seriously the belonging groups of the person who seeks help and the effect identification with those belonging groups has for the experience and behavior of that person.

6

THE TASK OF INTEGRATION

Paul, a social worker from a country in northern Europe, has volunteered to work in Asia for a few years, and he is nearing the conclusion of his overseas term. He has become friends with a young Javanese woman named Siti who is suffering from tuberculosis. Siti grew up in central Java as a Muslim, which means that her understanding of her religion is very much influenced by the legends of Hinduism and traditional Javanese values. Her belief system is characterized by an acceptance of suffering and a rather passive or at times fatalistic view of future events. Good and bad arrive in continuous progression as if they were part of a great wheel of time. She believes she has no control over the future, that is, she operates with an external locus of control (see chapter 4). She believes there is order to the universe, that divine powers are at work in a fragile cosmos, and that to rebel against the way things are in this world and the life beyond would invite the ire of the those powers and threaten to disturb cosmic harmony. Thus suffering must be borne patiently. Siti has similar attitudes about human relations. Javanese culture demands conflict avoidance and the perpetuation of communal harmony at all times, even though inside the apparently dormant volcano of community life the hot lava of conflict is boiling.

As much as he was enamored by the harmonious and gentle ways of the Javanese, Paul had much trouble with the placid acceptance of suffering he witnessed. He wanted the patients to scream and yell and rebel. He wanted them to taunt their fate, bowl it over with the sheer noise of their protests. He especially wanted this for Siti, for her fate was hardest to accept for him. Here was an attractive and innocent young woman his age who had two small children, an unemployed estranged husband, and a mother who sells rags at the nearby market: a woman who lives in a hut woven from bamboo, where the light of the sun is only visible through the cracks in the wall: a woman who is patiently and complacently coughing her way to an early grave. Paul came to Asia believing that the fate of people could be changed through commitment but found himself staring helplessly into the face of the inevitable. Once or twice he tried to feed her his anger:

"But don't you get angry?"

Siti: "I get frustrated. But what good does it do? I can't change anything."

Paul: "But you can fight harder."

Siti: "But why fight? It won't change anything. Everything has been decided."

Paul's attitude created a dilemma for Siti. On the one hand, she had to accept whatever life offered her, but on the other, she wanted to please this foreigner who wished for her to be a certain way. For the Javanese to accept what life hands you is a virtue expected of all. But it is also a virtue not to offend another person for the sake of harmony.

During one of her prolonged stays at the hospital, Siti was told that the landlord was going to evict them from their shack to make way for a lucrative building project. Finding a new place was not totally impossible, but it would take Siti's mother out of walking range from the market where she sold rags. It was already almost too far to walk, and the fare for a bicycle taxi would cancel out the possible earnings for the day. The clouds hung more heavily above Siti all the time. Not long afterwards, her two children were tested for tuberculosis and were diagnosed as also carrying the disease. The only bright light was the knowledge that her husband, who had been in prison for petty thievery, would be released in the forseeable future.

Siti did not overcome the disease. The hospital treatment somewhat strengthened her physically, but she was so emaciated that she lost the battle for her lungs. The hospitalizations were endless, and the separations were increasingly painful for her children until they were also diagnosed as positive. Then they were freer to visit.

Siti had become a Christian a year or so earlier, attracted by the caring of some members of the local congregation. However, she had never been fully assimilated into the church community. She was still a marginal member of the congregation, mostly unaware of its teachings. In a similar way she was a marginal member of her society, because she was a villager who had lived in the city most her life, without connections and with too little education to help her find employment.

When providing pastoral care, Paul was deeply troubled by her resignation and the hopelessness of the situation, as well as by his own helplessness. It was counter to his optimistic nature.

THE MANY FACETS OF SUFFERING

Siti's story shows pastoral care and counseling at its most complicated perhaps, assuming the caregiver is not resigned just to being with her instead of trying to change her life and reduce her suffering. Yet Siti's story is typical in pastoral care of the poor. A caregiver may be intent on making an impact on the mental state of the person but instead will be overwhelmed by anxiety and anger over the other's inability to feed his or her children or to find affordable housing. But the price of poverty is higher still. Relationships deteriorate and crime becomes more tempting. To truly help Siti, a caregiver would have to use a team approach involving doctors, nurses, social workers, community development workers, and other professionals, for so many aspects of her life lead to fragmentation and despair that the assistance of one kind of professional will not suffice. This means that an effective referral procedure is imperative for a caregiver who works with the poor. Whatever is said about Siti's suffering, we must understand that pastoral care is not complete without an evaluation of her economic and physical situation, as well as the relationship between those aspects of her life and her mental and spiritual condition. However, our discussion must naturally be limited to the aspects most relevant to pastoral care and counseling.

Worldview, identity, and sense of belonging were explored earlier. The task in this chapter is to explain more fully how worldview, identity, and sense of belonging function dynamically in the lives of people and how the task of integration of those three categories may be achieved.

THE PASTORAL CHALLENGE

Paul faces a number of difficulties. He is a male, the same age as Siti, who visits her at her bedside in the hospital. In Asia, this is not a situation conducive to intense conversation in which the patient confides in the chaplain. In addition, there is the problem of language. The two speak Indonesian, but Siti uses many Javanese terms and colloqualisms easily misunderstood by Paul. In addition, Paul could show more respect for her identity as a Javanese woman. Her identity moves her to act a certain way, play a certain role. She must be accepting, controlled, polite. Also, he needs to understand how strong her sense of belonging is as a Javanese and how this impels her to hold on to her worldview with devotion. Then there are also misunderstood cultural codes, misread nonverbal behavior that further complicate the encounter. Thus all the awareness, skills, and insight explored so far are needed for Paul to minister appropriately to Siti. He comes to her with a worldview that stipulates that we must fight against suffering and death, that says we must speak our minds, that allows a person to shake a fist at existence and so, maybe, just maybe, be healed.

PEOPLE FROM A WHOLISTIC PERSPECTIVE

Siti does not have a clear inner conflict between current identity, sense of belonging, and/or worldview such as those we have detected in some of the other care seekers we have met thus far. Her childhood identity is affirmed by her present identity, which in turn is consonant with her sense of belonging, which again is in harmony with her Javanese worldview.

Christian theology, of which she still knows very little, has not done much to discredit her Javanese philosophy of life. Her problem as she sees it is that she is caught in a web of fate. The future has been determined and there is nothing she can do to change her destiny. Theology affirming divine predestination of worldly events would encourage her to acquiesce. Outwardly, at least, she does, weakened by tubercular onslaught. Perhaps inwardly she does, too. But to Paul it is almost as if she were an observer of her own story, the victim but not as a participant. But then, to her, the idea that she has the freedom or power to change anything would appear rather absurd, for Siti believes she has no control over anything. In fact, she may not only think she has no control; she has none. She has no control over where her family might move to, when her husband comes home from prison, whether her children have tuberculosis or will eat, whether her mother can find another job. All she can do is pray and hope and fight. But she will not fight. Because fighting will disturb the harmony and balance of the cosmos. And if she believes that harmony is disturbed by her rebelliousness, all of Java will frown on her and her misery will grow even deeper. Siti obeys the standards her belonging groups have instilled in her, including all the values and restrictions of her environment. She can only live up to the age-old Javanese principles of *pasrah* (to be resigned) and *nrimo* (to bear) and accept her fate gracefully. The entire amalgam of her three stories (worldview, identity, sense of belonging) tell her it must be so.

So Paul gazes perplexed at Siti's worldview, marvels at her patience and tolerance, and despairs at her unwillingness to fight her disease to the bitter end or to a new beginning. He is interested in her emotions, and his search for the deeply hidden "no" he feels she must harbor is probably a mystery to her, or an entertaining diversion, or both.

Had Paul pursued his client-centered counseling approach, as a pastoral authority he would have created a formidable threat to her worldview and consequently to her identity and sense of belonging. What Paul failed to realize is that somehow there is meaning for Siti, for in tolerating graciously what is sent her way, she performs according to her world's expectations. Harmony is not disturbed. Her culture and her personality perfectly reflect each other.

SITI'S LIFE IN A WHOLISTIC PERSPECTIVE

The major problem for people who live in a pluralistic setting is that they tend to have too many models for being and behaving to work with. This can lead to real confusion, for often worldview can be in conflict with identity, or identity with sense of belonging, or sense of belonging with worldview. Having many models can also lead to internal discrepancies of identity, sense of belonging, and worldview. We have seen such internal discrepancies in James, Asmarat, David, Musa, and Judy in the preceding chapters. In contrast, it is helpful to consider human experience in a relatively homogeneous context, where these kind of incongruencies are not as likely to appear. For this we turn to the example of Siti's main cultural group, the people of central Java.

We can distinguish between two groups of people in central Java, the people in the village and the *priyayi* of the city, who are better educated and worldly and have closer ties to the Sultan's palace, meaning that traditionally they are related to the aristocracy or servants of the aristocracy. Many of the *priyayi* are now government employees. The worldliness of these people comes to expression, among other ways, in their ability to speak the three different levels of Javanese and to keep them separate. As explained earlier, there is one level spoken to children, subordinates and close friends. The middle level is used for polite conversations with acquaintances of similar stature. The third level is meant only for superiors and respected older people. The villagers are often considered *kasar* or rough/coarse, because they do not employ the languages in an appropriate fashion. Among the Javanese another major distinction can be made between the devout Muslims or *santri* and the majority *abangan* whose Javanese identity is stronger than their Muslim identity.

Different layers of worldview have become part of Javanese culture. The first layer is mostly characterized by ancestor worship and mysticism. This mysticism lives on in legends such as the one about a widely loved and feared goddess of the Indian Ocean. The second layer is Hinduism, which has yielded the legends of the Mahabharata and Ramayana that are very much alive in the popular shadow puppet performances. The third layer is Buddhism, whose short-lived reign has produced Borubudur, one of the world's largest religious monuments. Finally, Islam arrived, becoming the dominant religion. For Siti, of course, the fifth layer, Christianity, has become part of her worldview recently.

Some of the pervasive Javanese principles are *hormat, rukun* and *alus*. The first denotes respect or honor that one adheres to in relation to superiors and older people. The second is the principle of harmony and unity of the cosmos, which touches even all relationships. This underlies Siti's reluctance to defy her fate. The harmony of the cosmos should not be challenged. The Sultan is central to that cosmos, holding a divine power that is not earned but granted and removed at will by cosmic powers. The last principle is generally considered to be most clearly demonstrated by the palace inhabitants and servants. It is the opposite of rudeness and is best described as an almost aloof politeness, a calmness and smoothness that hides any negative experience or feelings of exuberance.

The principles of Javanese life are most lucidly affirmed by palace life in two royal cities. These palaces consist of large compounds or small towns in the heart of the city, where customs are so powerful that the continual waves of tourism or even centuries of colonial rule have had virtually no effect. The Javanese do take over ideas and customs from other cultures, but these ideas and cultures are harmoniously, albeit syncretically, integrated into the existing culture. Thus the culture has the appearance of homogeneity and harmony.

For the inhabitants, a clear identity exists. They know precisely their position and role in the present and the future. Every detail of the customs prescribed is taught to them as children. Their sense of belonging is stable and tied into their self-concept. Frames of reference are all shared. Theirs is an official "implicit" politeness code. The stories from the Mahabharata and Ramayana offer a plethora of opportunities for identification. In fact, the characters provide official personality types. They share the heroic accounts about the ancestors of the region's legends. Rules for courtship and marriage have been laid down with tedious attention to detail.

If a person experiences acute personal difficulties, the person is referred to the moral codes, so there is no doubt about the action that needs to be taken. Therefore identity, sense of belonging, frame of reference all rotate around the same well-known identifications. Of course, when this society comes in contact with threatening values, dissonance occurs, but so far the culture has been able to neutralize influences by blending them in, although the tediousness of the rituals is causing more and more impatience among the locals.

Javanese caregivers in the palace have a wealth of resources at their fingertips: similar identity, shared sense of belonging, shared frame of reference, shared identifications, shared symbols. These concepts function in relative harmony, affirming and strengthening each other. However, the moment care seekers move away from this setting and add new experiences to their frame of reference, the caregiving context becomes intercultural.

Siti is Javanese; that part of her identity is clear. But her sense of belonging as a full-fledged member of society is impaired because she does not have the resources to live up to the expectations of a proper Javanese woman. Her worldview is very much Javanese. So in a sense, her identity and worldview are in a slight tension with her sense of belonging because of the socioeconomic limitations she lives with. The result is a sense of inferiority and a feeling of resignation that never caught Paul's attention because of the domination in his mind of his own worldview.

THE WHOLE PERSON AND DIAGNOSIS

Our discussion has clear practical implications. If worldview, identity, and belonging in their interrelationship are indeed essential, they should be included in any cross-cultural pastoral care model. One of the first phases described by any helping model is the diagnostic phase, and it is in this phase that these concepts or categories are most needed.

Caregivers and situations may differ with respect to the most appropriate diagnostic emphasis or emphases, but I believe the three categories have clear diagnostic value. The causes of problems can be examined quite comprehensively by focusing on the interaction between sense of belonging, identity, and worldview. In addition, the incongruence that becomes apparent between worldview, identity, and sense of belonging can point to a new way of viewing a problem. Also, through that search, the tension between dissonant worldviews can be mitigated. The systematic yet subtle attention given by the pastor to parishioners and their problems can lay bare the fragmentation and brokenness of these persons and lead both pastor and parishioner toward a more whole-making interaction.

IDENTIFICATION AS DYNAMIC PRINCIPLE

When moving to a framework for cross-cultural pastoral care and counseling, it is important to present a unifying principle that will strengthen that framework and make it consistent. That principle is identification. Identification will be the yarn that unites those topics for the caregiver and the care seeker and continuously gives the caregiver clues about how to continue the pastoral care and counseling encounter. It helps when establishing diagnosis, but it also binds caregiver and care seeker across boundaries of meaning. It can simply be defined as "seeing something of oneself in another."

Identification does not only occur with respect to people with prominent or leadership roles in society, community, and the family, but also in relationship to perceived equals.

As their cultural processes develop, so do the images people live by and with which they identify, images that are to a great extent the result of other identifications.

Identification is an important state of mind and a condition for interpathy. Pastors must see themselves in parishioners in order to move across cultural barriers. Pastors must see something of the other in themselves, and vice versa. This principle is at the heart of intercultural and interracial conflict and suspicion: One group is not able to see itself in the other. They see only something alien and therefore frightening. Identification and consequently interpathy is intentional. It means the willingness to be united in common experience. However, not all identification is intentional. In response to certain people, a person may experience spontaneous identification. And not all spontaneous identification is healthy. For instance, it can lead to involvement in gangs or groups that offer destructive religious experiences. Helping professionals warn against overidentification with people in need of help, because the helper may be adversely affected or swept away with the emotion of those persons. They recommend that the caregiver retain an emotional distance, and these are legitimate words of warning. Nevertheless, intentional identification is of great importance in cross-cultural pastoral care and counseling. While in the interaction with persons of similar cultural backgrounds, empathy may seem to be a relatively routine and largely cognitive exercise, this is certainly not true of interpathy. Crossing cultural barriers requires a certain commitment to going over and above, to entering an alien world. It is tempting to try to touch the other person from one's own place across the chasm of meaning, but it is difficult to operate in different worlds at the same time. Thus identification becomes a temporary crossing over, and interpathy means seeing the world through very different eyes. It can be as dangerous and toilsome as it is enriching. The encounter with Siti should suffice as an example.

As explained in chapters 4 and 5, sense of belonging is very much dependent on identification with a group. It follows that worldview also plays an important role. For if the worldview held by a group to which a person wishes to belong is antithetical to that person's currently held worldview, identification will not take place as easily. Shared worldview can stimulate identification. Not all caregiving relationships are characterized by shared religious worldview, but there usually is an opportunity to discover some common ground in worldview through the exploration of the care seeker's and caregiver's frames of reference.

Personal identity is largely determined by a series of identifications. Once core identity has developed, continuous identification with friends, leaders, spouses, pastors, sports heroes, and others who influence people can contribute to self-redefinition.

This brings us to sense of belonging. Identification can strengthen a person's sense of belonging if his or her identifications are acceptable in the belonging group. In addition, sense of belonging can make identification more meaningful if connections can be made between the object or focus of identification and the belonging group. Identification and sense of belonging are closely allied in combatting alienation, for they both contrast with it.

There is a spiritual dimension to this question. For instance, as the worshiping community comes together, its members are united in a bond that ultimately transcends their differences. Through joint identification with the divine, they affirm that they not only belong to the God they worship, but on a deep level, they belong to each other. This identification and belonging can be tapped by a caregiver, who can assist the care seeker in finding appropriate belonging groups, whether that includes a church community or not.

If the care receiver has a strong sense of belonging in communities where the caregiver is not at home, the caregiver should make efforts not to threaten the person's existing sense of belonging.

People need continuous identification, and they need a constant sense of belonging in order to function in fullness. To help care seekers gain or regain a sense of belonging is, I believe, an important part of pastoral care and counseling.

Now how can the principle of identification be beneficial in the practice of cross-cultural pastoral care and counseling? First, it is important to understand that even though culture, worldview, identity, and sense of belonging are inseparable in people's lives, identification enhances these areas *simultaneously*. It is through identification that worldview can be strengthened in human relationships. It is through identification with other people that identity is determined and evolves. It is through identification that sense of belonging is strengthened. It is through identification that persons move from one meaning providing process to another.

Second, identification unites care giver and care seeker as they recognize themselves in each other and interpathy is born. When discussing understanding people who are very different from us, Anthropologists use the term "experimental mind reading" (Geertz 1973, 357), but identification goes beyond that. It offers not so much the experimental mind but the *experimental heart*.

The task of the caregiver is to keep an eye on the identifications care seekers bring to the encounter. Do these identifications contradict each other? If they do, there should be an attempt to bring these conflicting identifications into dialogue and wholeness with each other. At any point in life, human beings are besieged by the forces that drive them to brokenness and fragmentation. Tensions and internal dissonance result. A person's self-concept will move him or her in a certain direction, but the person's worldview may push another way. A person's sense of belonging again leads to another place. I have stressed that because of the vulnerability of the care receiver, the caregivers should try to avoid threatening worldview, identity, and sense of belonging.

The discussion above leads us to the following principle: The cross-cultural caregiver should help care seekers integrate or reintegrate worldview, identity, and sense of belonging by focusing on identification processes in the care seeker's life and by intentionally identifying through interpathy with the care seeker.

7

THE BIBLICAL STORY AS
RESOURCE

Sharon is an African American woman who seeks help at a pastoral counseling center affiliated with a church. Martin, a young European American, is assigned to be her counselor. They have four counseling sessions together.

Sharon moved two years ago from another city and still has not quite adjusted to the new surroundings. Before that, she had moved three times during the twelve years she has been married. She says she has a hard time trying to decide where her home is. But she claims that the reason for her coming to see a counselor is her relationship with her husband. Her husband, Jerald, is the son of a minister and feels strongly about his involvement in the church. Since they arrived in town, they have joined a church, where Jerald has started to spend more and more time. Most nights after work, Jerald devotes much of his time to the church, conducting the choir or leading Bible studies. This has forced Sharon to take on more of the parenting role than previously. The domestic role and the lack of attention from her husband occasionally cause her to suffer from depression. It is as if she does not exist for him. To add to her troubles, she feels Jerald is much too popular with the women in the choir. They often sing his praises to her, telling Sharon what a good looking, charming, and talented man her husband is. Sharon feels herself growing insignificant as Jerald shines. Each week their relationship appears to deteriorate a little more.

Sharon really seems to enjoy the counseling sessions. They talk about the things that have happened around the house: "Yesterday he came home at eight and wanted to know where his dinner was. He was real short and all. As if I owed it to him. I said, 'Honey, you've got two hands, why don't you get it. Can't you see I'm ironing.' He said he didn't understand why the ironing took me all day long, because he went to work, ate on the run, and then worked at church. And then I said, 'Yeah, you run the church to have your ego stroked by those well-dressed girls who complement you on your wonderful talent and your nice smile and your booming voice.' Then he yells at me and says he can't believe I'm jealous. So I tell him that I'm not jealous, but that I used to teach music, that I have a music degree from college, but no, they want Jerald and his smile and his baritone. 'You come home and expect dinner. What am I? A doormat you wipe your shiny shoes on, *honey*?!' "

Martin's discomfort with the counseling process increases as he sees no movement toward problem resolution. He has used a client-centered approach so far, which has given Sharon ample opportunity to talk. Finally he suggests that for the next session both Sharon and Jerald come to see Martin. Jerald, who has approved of Sharon going to counseling, immediately agrees to come. During this session Martin is very impressed by Jerald, his friendliness and poise, but nevertheless he gives equal attention to Jerald and Sharon. During the session, Jerald's responses are articulate and lengthy. Sharon's responses are brief and subdued. After the session, Martin never hears from them again and is convinced of his failure.

STORIES IN PASTORAL CARE AND COUNSELING

Martin faces the challenge of understanding why Sharon and Jerald never returned, but has no framework that he shares with them from which to approach the issue.

Frame of reference is a concept that has been mentioned a number of times. It is the reservoir for experiences, knowledge, and values used to fashion and refashion one's worldview. Stories are part of frame of reference. For the interaction that takes place in the pastoral context, sacred stories, biblical stories, are an important part of people's frame of reference. In cross-cultural pastoral care, we long for at least a partially shared frame of reference. Biblical stories provide that partially shared frame of reference that informs the worldview of both care seeker and caregiver.

Is it appropriate to use stories in pastoral care and counseling? To answer this question, identification must again be mentioned. Stories provide a wealth of analogics to human lives. Stories make it possible for human beings to see the story characters as metaphors and symbols of their own lives. The listeners or readers can be struck by the realization that "Yes, that character is a bit like me." In other words, the story allows them to identify. This kind of identification can often be less painful and more enriching than identifying with someone who is non-fictional, for it is easier to say, "That character isn't really me. It's just a story, after all." It is a self-transcending type of identification, identification with an escape valve. Nevertheless, it can be meaning producing. In addition, the language of the story has poetic power; it evokes something, rather than explains. For this reason, many therapists utilize stories in counseling. They hit the reader and the listener in a very unique place, jarring loose emotions and creating images that can lead swiftly to shifts of perspective. Martin's challenge is to find a story that can be helpful to Sharon. This is difficult, because Martin has had almost no contact with African Americans.

IDENTIFICATION AND THE SACRED STORY

While stories are useful in caregiving, the religious story adds another dimension. This dimension lies in the power of the religious story to give someone the chance to identify with a character who stands in close relationship to the divine, thereby strengthening and enabling subjective individual religious experience. Again, identification is important.

The religious story character becomes a mirror to people, revealing feelings of which they were not yet aware. Also, the religious story can help a person attain self-transcendence, for the realization that the person with whom the care seeker identifies has had experiences analogous to the care seeker's helps widen horizons and relativizes suffering. At the same time, the unique relationship between the story character and the divine stengthens the care seeker's own belonging within the divine. The self-transcendence also strengthens the care seeker's sense of togetherness with those who hear the story with him or her.

Edward Wimberly advocates a "narrative" approach in pastoral care with African Americans such as Sharon:

Since we assume that storytelling is the basic method of learning within the black culture, the implication is that black pastors must be able to reflect on the stories they tell, for the purpose of visualizing their healing value for the themselves and others. They must have a setting in which they can tell stories to one another and, through this sharing, resolve personal anxiety as well as become conflict-free in their own minds (Wimberly 1991, 82).

Wimberly further explains that storytelling in pastoral counseling has proved very helpful in his counseling. For example, he tells the story of a parishioner with a very negative outlook on life who was burdened by many painful memories. Wimberly retold to him the story of Joseph, as it is read first by one person who stops reading at the moment Joseph is sold into slavery, and then by another reader who continues reading through the account of Joseph's eventual triumph (Wimberly 1991, 100–104). Retelling the Joseph story was designed to lift the care seeker's spirits through identification with the Joseph character. The person takes over the role of Joseph, who is an important figure in the history of the people of God. Thus the person can transcend the darkness of his present experience and view a larger expanse of his life with a new perspective.

The approach of biblical storytelling is not only useful in the pastoral care of African Americans. Musa mentioned to Bill at one point (see chapter 4) that he felt like Jonah, who runs away from the responsibility of everyday life. The more people move between cultural processes and the more their once clear frames of reference and worldviews blur, the more the symbolically powerful biblical story with its stabilizing impact and its agelessness becomes a valuable resource. Martin's challenge is to address Sharon's life with a story that speaks to her suffering. This does not mean that the biblical story has to fit over Sharon's life exactly, or even that it has to be the story of a woman. All that is necessary is that a fragment or fragments of her life temporarily overlap with a fragment or fragments of the story character's life so that in an instant of identification, a new pain-transcending perspective is born. This dynamically hermeneutical moment becomes the starting point for a dialogue— with Martin mostly listening and responding—leading to change. The use of the sacred story has implications for the different aspects of people's life. Through identification with the story character, the worldview of faith is affirmed, identity as a child of God is affirmed, and sense of belonging in the believing community is deepened.

ENCOUNTER AND BIBLICAL STORY

Now that it has been determined that the sacred story can be used in cross-cultural pastoral care and counseling, the question of matching the stories of parishioner and biblical character, as well of pastor, needs to be addressed. What really happens? Martin or Sharon suggests a story he or she sees as analogous to the situation, experiences, or character of the counselee. As such a "matching up" takes place, the experience of care seeker and story character become analogous to or metaphoric for one another. There is no exegetical method that can be used in this matching. That would involve a toilsome integration of psychological and anthropological analysis and biblical interpretation. Even if this were possible, it would be too time consuming. The key again is identification. Martin sees something of himself in Sharon; perhaps he sees her loneliness, the fact that she is rather introverted, the fact that she does not feel totally at home, a lack of confidence, or a sense of self-pity. Instead of trying to label her experience and interpret it from his worldview, he enters the realm of their shared frame of reference, the biblical story. Through his identification with her and through the consequent interpathy, he recognizes something of himself in her that he also sees in a sacred story character and he says, "What you are telling me brings to mind the story of Ruth, who gives up the security of her world to follow her husband." Sharon may respond, "But I have no mother-in-law, and I hope I'm not going to lose my husband." The dissimilarity can be as useful as the similarity. She may continue, "But it's true that I have followed my husband and have been loyal to him." Undramatically, a meeting of lives, the joining of stories, is taking place. A meeting point has been discovered. It may be momentary or it may open the door to lengthy conversations that last several sessions. If the dissimilarities greatly outweigh the similarities, Martin can encourage Sharon to suggest a story that reflects her life. They may jump from story to story, selecting fragments of characters' lives to form a picture. This may be possible in her case, because she knows the sacred stories well. With another care seeker, some stories may have to be retold or read together first.

There are a number of stories that may speak to Sharon. The Joseph story mentioned above is one example. They could focus on the fact that his dark moments in the well and the prison experience are not permanent. Again, Ruth's loyalty could be a starting point for joint reflection. The idea of the promised land is another area to be explored. What are her ideals for her life and her family, and is there a point of contact with journeys of Abraham and Sarah and Moses? Then again, she may have questions about her suffering that are similar to those Job had. Even the story of the prodigal may provide an analogy: Will she accept her husband back into an intimate relationship after he has taken for granted the gift of her abiding love? The selection of stories should be carried out with reference to the following three criteria:

- the degree to which, in the care seeker's perception after joint interpretation, his or her situation and problems are analogous to the situation and problems of the story character;
- the degree to which the care seeker can accept the personality aspect in the story character as interpreted;
- the extent to which the care seeker can accept the experiences of the story character as analogous to his or her own.

The above translates into the following principle: The caregiver should make creative use of the biblical story with care receivers who know the stories or who are open to them, in order to tap the story's metaphoric power through identification.

8

FAMILY PASTORAL CARE
ACROSS CULTURES

Elena and Manuel are a Mexican American couple experiencing marital difficulties. Elena works long hours as a nurse in a downtown hospital. Her work hours are irregular. Sometimes she works evenings, at other times mornings or the night shift. Manuel co-owns a car repair shop that has fallen on hard times. They have four children, ranging in age from eleven to four years. Elena's parents were born in the United States and are now deceased (her mother more recently), but Manuel's parents live in Sonora state in Mexico.

Every year the whole family travels south for a family reunion for two weeks. Elena does not enjoy these vacations, for she would rather go to a place she has never seen before. Also, it seems Manuel's and Elena's relationship always deteriorates right after the holiday, and the discussion often begins on the long drive home. Elena is convinced that Manuel's parents indoctrinate him about how the two of them should relate to each other. Manuel denies that. The discussion mostly centers around their roles in the households. Manuel and his family appear to believe that Elena should spend more time with the children and be there when the children come home from school. Manuel takes care of the children on the days Elena is working the evening shift. On the other hand, he acknowledges that the income Elena brings in is crucial to the family's economic survival, since his income is currently very limited.

Elena feels guilty about not spending much time with the children, but she and her coworkers (who make up a culturally diverse group) seem to be in the same situation. She does get tired, but her fatigue seems to be offset by her dedication to her work.

Lately the argument over parental roles has widened into arguments about the frequency of sexual relations, the family budget, and doubts about the couple's feelings for each other.

After mass one sunday, Elena approached the local Roman Catholic priest, explaining that Manuel has been really depressed lately and that he should probably speak to a priest. The priest, a European American named Jim O'Connor, asked Elena to elaborate on Manuel's depression and after further information from Elena concluded that the heart of problem lay in their relationship and not in Manuel's attitude. He then suggested they both come to the church for counseling.

Both Elena and Manuel were amiable and cooperative during the first meeting. Jim could detect no great animosity between the two and concluded that they both still very much loved each other. They spoke to each other affectionately and genuinely.

However, during the second meeting, an argument developed between Elena and Manuel as Manuel was speaking full of affection about his mother in Mexico. Elena interrupted him and blurted out some negative comments about her mother-in-law. This ignited Manuel: "Don't talk about your mother-in-law that way! Do you want the father to think you are not a good Catholic!" Elena snapped back: "Don't you tell me I'm not a good Catholic!" I give myself to my patients and family while all you do is complain!"

Manuel: "Your patients, of course, your patients come first. We are second. Your patients always come first."

Elena: "What! How can you say that? I still do all the cooking, and I don't see you cleaning the house. And who comes first in your life, huh, your wife and children, or that old manipulating mama of yours? I have no parents anymore. I only have you to support me, and a great job you are doing!"

Jim, realizing their argument was coming full circle in a very short time, asks Manuel's permission to turn to Elena for a few minutes, since she appears more distraught at this moment. Manuel agrees.

Jim: "Elena, what is upsetting you the most right now?"

After a period of silence she answers: "I just don't feel appreciated. I work hard, I care about people, I come home and work in the house. On my days off, I help my children with their school work, I go to the store . . . So why am I so bad? I am trying to live my life the best I can. I feel so lonely sometimes."

Manuel interjects (sounding moved): "But why feel lonely? You have me and the kids."

Elena: "Yes, I know. But it's as if no one understands me anymore."

Jim: "Why do you say 'anymore,' Elena? Was there anyone who could?"

After a prolonged silence Elena begins to cry: "Yes, yes, my mother. I miss my mother . . ."

Both Manuel and Elena feel jealous. Elena is jealous of Manuel because he still has a mother, and of Manuel's mother because she and her youngest son are so close. Manuel is jealous of Elena's coworkers at the hospital for making her too "American," too independent from her husband, too much of a "working woman." They both want more attention from each other, but they feel attention is being withheld, and as a result they withhold their love even more.

Marital counseling is complex and dangerous enough as it is without it being done cross-culturally. But Jim O'Connor truly wants to understand the world of this Latino American couple. Furthermore, he has to understand each of these people who feel partially shut out of each other's world. He does not want to alienate either one of them by favoring the other. He must be a friend to both.

Manuel and Elena are both frustrated. A number of their needs or wants are not being met. Manuel wants Elena to be a more traditional mother who will be mindful of the needs of the children and of his sexual needs. At the same time, his needs to be successful in his career are not being met. Because he is not successful—his business is failing—more of a demand is put on him to take over some of Elena's traditional responsibilities. Therefore the frustration about one need feeds the frustration about others.

The problems Manuel and Elena face are far from uncommon. The pressure of economic hardship, the changing roles of men and women in marriages, the influence of parents in the lives of their children of any age, are known to many in differing degrees across cultural lines. Therefore Jim as an experienced caregiver is not likely to be caught off guard by their story. The symptoms are similar to the ones he has seen many times during his years in the ministry. While this puts him in a position to help, however, it also puts him at a distinct disadvantage. Jim is likely to view the problems confronted by this Mexican American couple in much the same way he would a couple with a cultural background similar to his own. Therein lies a danger, for one of the first things he must learn when providing cross-cultural pastoral care is that understanding the nature of the problem is less important than understanding what the problems mean to the persons who experience them. Therefore Jim must be aware that the depth and breadth of meaning that events and problems evoke varies across cultures no matter how similar they may seem.

Even if Jim realizes that problems mean different things to different people, there is a related predicament he faces, namely recognizing cultural subtleties behind the words and behavior of Elena and Manuel. So much of the information available concerning other cultures and religions is theoretical and academic. The books on the subject are more focused on historical trends and philosophical traditions than aimed at understanding how historical fragments and vestiges of tradition blend and clash in people as they shape their lives in a pluralistic age. We may be struck by Elena and Manuel's eloquence and see in them a mainstream North American couple. This impression would be both true and false. Yes, they are an average couple, but their culture is not as mainstream as it may seem, and that culture has bearing on the problems they confront.

Another issue that needs to be addressed is that of the possibility of overemphasizing the couple's cultural background. Manuel and Elena are both Mexican American. They both speak English, and they both speak Spanish. Manuel had lived with an uncle in the United States since he was very small, all the while remaining close to his parents, whom he would see annually. Therefore it is not easy to classify Elena and Manuel as Mexican American, much less as Latino American, for these are not homogenous groups. Yet Jim may not sufficiently recognize that Manuel and Elena bring a subtle mixture of cultural influences, despite their own understanding and the understanding of most others that they are Mexican Americans or Latino Americans.

Related to this, the next significant question that needs to be addressed pertains to the cultural gap between Elena and Manuel themselves. Jim may be convinced by their cultural similarities that their cultural *dis*similarities are negligible. He can be tempted to think that way because we tend to paste labels on population groups. More often than not, we tend to delineate population groups with wide brushstrokes, referring to groups such as Latino Americans, Arab Americans, or Native Americans as homogenous cultural entities, not to mention our even more generalizing categorization of "Asian Americans." Yet the nation of Indonesia alone harbors cultures as different from one another as can be found any place in the world.

Elena has been raised without the rather homogeneous influence of rural Mexican society. She has always been able to identify with a variety of ethnic groups. This experience is affirmed in the heterogeneous setting of the hospital where she works and is partially strengthened by the alienating impact of her mother-in-law, whom Elena considers to be a divisive force in the relationship between her and her husband.

Manuel has usually sought his friendships among Mexicans and Mexican Americans and still feels very much at home with his family in Mexico. He sees Elena as being in his cultural circle, even as he believes she is slowly slipping. He sees Elena's colleagues and friends as divisive.

What are the consequences of these factors for Jim's helping attempts? How can we translate them into guidelines for action in the cross-cultural encounter?

First, Elena and Manuel must be given the opportunity to present the problem as they see it. As Jim listens, he should search and probe for information that might shed light not only on the problems themselves but on the meaning these problems have for them. He can check this information against the background of the knowledge he has about their cultural community. Second, Jim should avoid approaching problems that appear common by glossing over the fact that different people have different reactions to these problems. Third, Jim must be conscious of the fact that Manuel and Elena's way of viewing each other's worlds is continuously in process.

Fourth, he must recognize that his way of viewing their problems and other problems is also in process, whether he is moving into new arenas or returning to earlier viewpoints. Jim needs to be conscious of his own ambivalence in this area.

Fifth, he must resist the temptation to force the information he receives from Elena and Manuel to conform to his theoretical perceptions of that background.

UNDERSTANDINGS OF MARRIAGE AND SEXUALITY

Understandings of the institution of marriage vary in different contexts. For some it is a sacred bond that cannot be severed at any time. For others it is an arrangement that opens the door to forming one's own nuclear family. This is why in some Asian countries, it is desirable for a couple to conceive a child as soon as possible after wedding vows are exchanged. If family planning programs are successful, the second and final child will be born years later, but the first child should come as soon as possible, so that the status of family is achieved. Many European Americans confuse marriage with infatuation and erotic attraction, and overload the marriage relationship with unrealistic expectations. In some cultures, promiscuity alongside marriage is quite customary, although when people are asked whether it is condoned, they may answer that it is not. In a large number of cultures the most important principle is that the family stays formally intact regardless of the quality of the marital relationship. In many cultures, marriage is a instrument by which clans are perpetuated or brought together and, as in north Sumatran societies in Indonesia, there may be clear rules about the precise kin relationships allowed and forbidden between candidates for marriage.

In Indonesia young people are often prohibited by their clans from marrying across cultures, but they may find it impossible to extricate themselves from the emotional relationship with someone from outside their cultural group. They often solve the problem by hanging on to the relationship as long they possibly can in an attempt to mollify the families. In the end, the families may realize that severing such a long relationship would be devastating for the children. Nevertheless, if a candidate has been chosen by the family and the match is useful to the continued peacefulness of the village, the young person may be forced to relent. This becomes an even more complex question when the relationship is interreligious. In countries with both large Christian and Islamic populations the dilemmas may be heartbreaking. Religious fervor is usually high, for both religions are highly proselytizing in nature, and people may have to choose between the person they love and the family they love.

Unless the community that the new couple settles in is relatively tolerant religiously and they themselves play down their religious differences, the question of religion will most certainly haunt them. The greatest difficulty will come when there are children, and the children, contrary to the couple's expectations, become the battleground of the faiths.

The expression of sexuality varies greatly between cultures. In some African cultures, sexuality is celebrated equally by men and women, but in others the custom of female circumcision continues. In many Asian cultures, women are to have a submissive role in sexual expression and are not expected to show great interest in sexual activity, since desire for sexual activity may be interpreted as showing the woman's potential for unfaithfulness. In most cultures the man is favored in sexuality, work, and responsibility for supporting the home. The caregiver will find variety in the degree to which people accept these roles.

The question of homosexuality does not create the tenseness in every culture that it does in most European Americans or among African Americans. Homosexuals may be accepted, although homosexuality is rarely preferred to heterosexuality. More often than not, homosexuals are considered a separate class of persons, but in a large number of cultures their sexual expression would not be threatening to heterosexual members of the same gender.

SELECTIVE VALUE CROSSOVER

In the cross-cultural marriage or relationship, partners are likely to try on the values of the other, at times becoming quite comfortable with those values. This apparent level of comfort and acceptance may create the impression that a person has discarded her or his own traditional values in a particular area, and that the change in values may be taken for granted. However, a person may revert back to the old values whenever it is suitable for the sake of argument. Manuel may suddenly be very "American" in outlook if is advantageous to him, for instance when he pushes his wife to express her sexuality in a more "modern" way in their relationship. On the other hand, he may expect her to quit her job when he has a stable one, because the mother is supposed to be at home as his mother was. In a similar way, Elena may expect Manuel to do the "male" jobs around the house, such as fixing broken appliances, while at the same encouraging him to do the household chores that are the traditional domain of the woman. I call this "selective value crossover." In marriage that is more starkly cross-cultural than theirs, crossover would be even more noticeable. Both partners at times confuse value issues that at other times they define clearly and rigidly. People's tendency to adopt new values also depends on their mood. People tend to be less rigid when they are relatively content. But the crossover may come back to haunt them in the next argument.

FAMILY COUNSELING

In most non-European cultures, particularly with Asian families, family counseling will be a difficult undertaking. Many cultures will not encourage a parent, especially the senior male in the family, to admit wrongdoing, so the family relationship in counseling is lopsided from the start. In many cases it will be impossible to get one or more family members to meet with the counselor. These family members, however, may be willing to speak face to face with the counselor and will make complaints about the behavior of other family members the focal point of the conversation. In many Asian nations the nature of the parent-child relationship does not leave much room for children to learn to make responsible decisions. Parents often are convinced that prematurely allowing responsibility will open the door to irresponsible behavior. Much of the conflict between parents and their children in contemporary Asian societies focuses on the childrens' demand to be taken seriously. A family counseling relationship where all the members are equal can be quite a difficult concept for the parents to adopt. However, in some Pacific cultures, routine family meetings meant to resolve interpersonal conflicts are quite common, thus providing a natural groundwork for family counseling.

Cross-cultural counselors may find themselves unable to arrange a much-needed family counseling session. I have found it helpful to invite family members to present their perspective one by one and to try to resolve conflicts as much as possible in that way. If that is not possible, a pastoral visit where the therapeutic and the social are mixed in a non-threatening fashion, can be quite productive. Families tend to feel stronger in a familiar environment. During moments of tension, inviting the family members to laugh at the counselor (for instance at the counselor's lack of knowledge of their culture) or at themselves can be quite helpful. The more family members have been exposed to other worldviews, the more cooperative they tend to be. While many cultures appreciate informality, caregivers' deliberate structuring of the counseling session, once the need for counseling is agreed to by all, will generally add to their status as professionals. People new to the practice of family counseling need to be reassured and calmed by the informal ways and the sense of humor of the counselor, but at the same time they want that counselor to be qualified and skilled. Otherwise they may feel they are wasting their time. Therefore a delicate balance must be struck.

The discussion above leads us the following principles:

- the caregiver must be aware that the cultures of family members can be in process at different paces and in different directions;
- understandings of marriage and sexuality differ greatly between cultures;
- selective value crossover can occur at any time in the family;
- in many cultures, there may be great resistance to family counseling, requiring a flexible strategy.

9

COUNSELING WITH SPECIFIC
CULTURAL GROUPS

The tendency to label and to categorize groups is not necessarily an asset to the cross-cultural caregiver, for it can lead the caregiver to press the experience of unique human beings into rigid categories. According to such categories, Manuel and Elena in the one of the previous chapters might belong in either the Latino American or Mexican American category. Yet Mexican Americans in south Texas are distinct from Mexican Americans in Los Angeles, who are particularly proud of having developed their own recognizable urban culture. In other words, the caregiver faces the danger of falling into the trap of placing the parishioners into frameworks shaped by presuppositions and information not obtained from the people themselves. Within cultural groups, there are many differences. This does not at all imply that learning about the general background of the people we counsel is not helpful. But it does mean that people tend to cross the cultural boundaries within which they are assumed to function exclusively. The task at hand is to counsel persons in their entirety, wholeness, and uniqueness, not to confine them within inflexible boundaries. Labels and categories tend to lead to a fragmented picture. Personhood tends to transcend cultural boxing. Yet we cannot deny that there are distinguishable cultural groups with much in common. In cross-cultural counseling literature, there are generally four major groups discussed, namely African Americans, Latino Americans, Asian Americans, and Native Americans. We can make several observations about this literature. First, the uniqueness of a variety of subgroups is not given appropriate attention. Second, it is presumed European Americans are the caregivers (since they are not discussed).

Finally, many groups such as Arab Americans, Jewish Americans, and Armenian Americans are not discussed separately. It is very difficult to be complete and consistent in treating such vast subject matter. However, it may be helpful to briefly present some of the major idiosyncrasies of the most often mentioned groups that are likely to show up in everyday practice.

African Americans suffer much from stereotyping. Racism often leads to an erroneous picture of African American men as excessively virile, irresponsible, artistic, athletic, and violent. Women are often alternately stereotyped as longsuffering victims of the behavior of men and as dependents of government services. Members of the majority cultural groups who do not know African Americans often view African Americans with a mixture of fear, guilt, and resentment. It is true that there are many single-parent families among African Americans, and that many African Americans live in poor, violent urban environments. In fact the greatest number of victims of violence by African Americans are African Americans themselves. The stereotyping has haunted all of African American history in North America and has made African Americans understandably suspicious of many people from other cultural groups, a factor that impedes cross-cultural counseling. In addition, caregivers from different cultural backgrounds are sometimes unable to dispel completely their primary culture's pervasive stereotype of African Americans. African American care receivers will often view the caregiver from another cultural background as part of a system that is automatically biased against them. Elsie Smith has recommended that the caregiver focus not only on the problems of the care seeker or even the family, but on the care seeker's social system (socio-therapy). In other words, counseling should also be career counseling and survival therapy, helping African American care receivers deal with a society they tend to experience as hostile (Sue 1981, 171–72). In such a society, a strong self-understanding is essential. Therefore it is important that the caregiver be open to discussing African American identity as distinct from their own. It is often helpful to address the discomfort that caregiver and care seeker feel in a cross-cultural counseling situation, especially if the caregiver is European American. I cannot overemphasize genuineness. On a number of occasions I have seen generally reserved European Americans abruptly change their behavior and become exuberant in the presence of an African American as a way of compensating for their lack of cross-cultural skills. African American care seekers, like all people who need help, above all need genuine caring. They understand that the cultural and historical chasm cannot be bridged by one awkward leap.

Native Americans can appear quite shy and quiet. Emotionally and spiritually they also live in two worlds, the world of the reservation and the world dominated by European Americans. Because over the past centuries they have been pushed to the margins of North American society and have suffered disproportionally, their self-confidence within that society is very low. Native Americans tend to be intrapunitive, meaning that they turn conflict inward. This partially explains high suicide rates among their groups.

For Native Americans, values and worldview are viewed wholistically. The idea of either/or is traditionally quite alien in the Native American community, where everything is one. Native Americans see nature and faith, animals, and the divine as aspects of the same sphere. Likewise, Native Americans can see apparently contradicting theologies, such as Mormon (LDS) and Presbyterian, as mutually complementary (Sue 1981, 223). Therefore it is not unusual for Native Americans to rotate their religious life by alternately attending a Pentecostal church, the traditional Protestant church established on the reservation many years ago, or the Mormon service, or by participating in ancient Native American ceremonies. A very high rate of alcoholism exists in the Native American community, with the bottle serving to fill the emptiness and despair so many Native Americans are born to. In spite of the quiet despair that lives below the surface on the reservation and that is carried to the outside, the dry sense of humor nurtured by suffering and the revitalized pride in the cultural traditions can become great resources to the caregiver. Out of fear of getting hurt, Native Americans are frequently cautious in relationships with outsiders to whom they actually feel drawn.

European Americans are usually not discussed because they are so often seen as the standard group from which all other groups deviate. European Americans often criticize other groups for "not blending in" well, for not being able to abandon their old cultural background for a new amalgamated "American" one. Frequently European Americans detect a certain arrogance in the cultural pride of others and believe that public institutions give minorities preferred treatment. They sometimes experience the strong cohesion of other groups as threatening, at the same time as they often long for such group cohesion themselves. There is much cultural flexibility for European Americans today because of the strong cultural commitment to the development of the individual's potential. The emphasis is often on removing obstacles to personal development and success. European Americans often display an extra-punitive attitude, blaming others rather than themselves of standing in the way of their personal fulfilment. Based on this worldview, often there are not enough reasons to perpetuate unsatisfying family relationships. Although European Americans value their commitments highly, they do believe that they should not thwart the individual's right to the pursuit of personal happiness. We will often find that European American care seekers are propelled by a myth that everyone can be happy and fulfilled. This myth is perpetuated by the entertainment industry, which is controlled by people who have a personal commitment to this myth, as well as to offering the European American majority the product they desire. In the counseling context, European Americans respond well to contracts, direct communication, and strong eye contact. Although they value privacy highly, they are able to abandon it at the appropriate time, such as in counseling. Counseling methodology as we know it has largely been based on the changing needs of the European American. We should be aware of the differences among European Americans, however, especially between those whose families came from the predominantly Protestant western and northern Europe and those whose families originated in the Roman Catholic- and Orthodox-dominated countries of the Mediterranean region. The latter groups tend to emphasize the role of the extended family more than the former, and those groups with a Roman Catholic background have much in common with Latino Americans. The values and attitudes of the nonorthodox Jewish communities are hard to distinguish from the values of the European American community as a whole, for they have blended their wordviews into worldviews that non-Americans may label as "typically American." This is also related to the fact that the ancestors of the majority of Jewish American families immigrated from European countries.

Latino Americans represent a mix of Native American peoples from the southwestern United States southward, as well as part of the Caribbean, and Europeans predominantly from the Iberian peninsula. In

North America the Native American influence tends to be dominant, but culturally there are many similarities between Spanish and Portuguese cultures.

In Latino cultures the cohesion of the family is very strong and is strengthened by Roman Catholic traditions prohibiting divorce and discouraging artificial birth control. This means that family problems must be worked out, or at least tolerated so as not to threaten the integrity of the family. The woman has a dominant role in the Latino family but will allow the man to be the official person in charge. The relationship between a son and his mother is of great significance and may eclipse the grown son's relationship with his spouse. The mother is likely to have a voice in most family matters after her son has married. Certain psychological interpretations suggest that the "macho" image and behavior of the Latino male is in fact compensation for the tender relationship with his mother (Wicks and Estadt 1993, 8). In counseling, the Latino woman will often be more vocal and verbal in expressing feelings, and appears to be more adept in adjusting to the majority cultures.

Asian Americans are a varied group. The Chinese Americans were one of the first groups to immigrate to the continental United States. Japanese Americans and Filipino Americans came much later to work in agriculture. Korean Americans have immigrated in large waves over the past decades. The Indo-Chinese came in the seventies and after. All groups emphasize the family. Filipino Americans in many ways are more similar to Latino Americans than to other Asian Americans because of the Spanish and American colonial history, and they seem to have little difficulty adapting to the majority cultures. Japanese Americans have an identity all their own. When they lost the ability to speak Japanese perfectly, they were not fully accepted by the "real" Japanese at home. At the same time, they were rejected by the majority cultures in the United States during the Second World War because they were of Japanese descent. This has meant double suffering for them. In spite of these obstacles, Japanese Americans are among the Americans who most successfully conform to the expectations of the majority culture but who yet do not have the comfort of a special relationship with the country of origin. As is the case with most Asian Americans, their drive to succeed is stronger than that of modern European Americans because a person succeeds foremost for his or her family. Family has religions connotations in the Buddhist tradition, although the term "ancestor worship" is somewhat misleading. They do not worship their ancestors; they revere, honor, and commune with them. Vietnamese Americans, Korean Americans, and Chinese Americans have strong bonds with their country of origin. This does not preclude them from being loyal citizens in the country to which they immigrate. But community transcends national boundaries, especially for the Chinese, who never really had diffculty defining what and where their nation was, as did the Vietnamese and Koreans as a result of the Korean and Viet Nam Wars. Asian Americans in general prefer a counselor who is polite, does not pry into areas that might cause them to feel shameful, and is professional and to the point. It is helpful to explain beforehand to the care seeker what the usual procedure is. The care seeker will most likely be cooperative but may not return once he or she has made a measurable amount of progress, or conversely, when he or she had made very little progress. To engage in prolonged counseling would require a delicate balance.

10

PASTORAL SELF-ASSESSMENT

Janine and John are co-pastors of a small, predominantly European American congregation in the suburbs of a large city. John has been a pastor for fifteen years, and Janine graduated from seminary two years ago. Janine and John consider themselves open in their outlook and very much aware of the newest developments in theology. They believe in moving congregations by both loving and socially challenging their members. European American members of the "baby boomer" generation, they have managed to raise two children, one to senior high and one to junior high age, while working and studying at the same time.

Janine and John believe they are more tolerant of cultural diversity than their parents were, and they were delighted when a Vietnamese American lay pastor started to attend their services. He mentioned that he had a dream of starting an outreach program and requested assistance from the congregation. The pastor proved to be quite successful in drawing Vietnamese Americans to the congregation. The number of families grew, and the congregation became a vibrant multi-cultural, albeit at times awkward, family. Janine and John did research diligently on Vietnamese culture, became devoted fans of Vietnamese cuisine, and fell in love with the friendly ways of the people themselves.

Over time, however, their enthusiasm was tested. The Vietnamese American community was allowed to use the church premises for a variety of social gatherings, but sometimes people in the neighborhood complained about large crowds and loud Vietnamese pop music. John and Janine were disturbed by the submissive role of many of the women and wondered what they could do to change that. Some of the women almost seemed a little afraid of their husbands. Furthermore, a few members of the original congregation reported seeing small altars used to honor the ancestors in the homes of some of the newer Vietnamese church members. Members had also heard a lot of talk about ghosts wandering through people's houses. Janine and John realized that these beliefs were centuries old and that they should not ridicule them, but they became aware that much of their intercultural tolerance was rather superficial.

In addition to these issues, Janine and John struggle with their responsibility to society. As committed as they are to social outreach, they fear rising crime in the cities and especially the violence in the schools. They want to roll up their sleeves and change society, but they also want to hide, find a comfortable nest in which to raise their family. They believe their children should not suffer on account of their parents' ideals. This was one of the factors in their decision to take a suburban church. As Janine and John struggle with their own identity, sense of belonging, and worldview, they try to formulate a vision for their church in a country where streets can go up in flames at any time and where they must reach out across cultural boundaries.

Janine and John have difficulty finding a balance between their instincts to protect their family, and their faith, which tells them they must reach out and identify with the poor and people from other cultures. On an emotional level, they find it hard to yield to this call to reach out, because of their own need for privacy, cultural expression, and family security.

Many pastors are interested in people who are different culturally. The excitement of different faces, accents, foods, ways of looking at life, the thrill of meeting people who practice religions we usually only read about or see on television is invigorating. But when working intensely with persons of different cultural backgrounds, irritation can definitely become part of the experience. After a while the entertaining cultural cuteness pales somewhat, and the universal weaknesses behind the custom become visible. We find there are limits to the worldview we are willing to accept, the frequency with which we are willing to eat strange foods, the patience we have for listening to people speak in incomprehensible tongues. Discovering these limits is as much a liberating as it is a difficult moment. For it is at this point that human beings can truly come face to face to assert their particularity. It is also the occasion for identification and interpathy, when we can become truly subject to the other.

Janine and John are struggling with their ambivalence. They strive to keep open minds, but they are reluctant to reach out with open hearts. What can they do? An important step in the right direction would be to commit themselves to not seeing their own cultural experience as a standard from which all other groups of people deviate, whether in a positive or a negative way. Thus they must place themselves in the margin, as visitors in the narthex.

Below we will be looking briefly at who Janine and John are culturally. The discussion can lead to an inventory for pastors to use to evaluate and understand themselves culturally and cross-culturally.

We begin with identity. John and Janine are baby boomers who came of age in the 1960s. They have created an image of themselves informed by their worldview. They are very much change oriented. The meaning providing processes of their time told them that the status quo was not acceptable, that the ways of their parents needed to be corrected. Of course, their parents were mystified. They had lived through the Second World War and had been grateful for the economic prosperity they could provide for their children, something their parents could not have dreamt of. John's and Janine's belief that change should be effected serves them well in their ministry. It makes them desirous of social justice and motivates them to try new approaches. Other cultures and religions proved attractive to their generation, which was a departure from the more homogenous culture of their parents. Thus, it was relatively easy for them to adopt an attitude of openness to people from other cultures such as the Vietnamese Americans.

Yet the worldview of their generation did not have deep roots, for it developed rapidly over a period of a decade, fading somewhat in the subsequent decades. Their decision to take on that worldview was not just an ethical choice, but it was born out of a desire to belong among their peers. They assumed they were the only ones who had reservations about so much passion for change, so much openness to experimentation, so much anger at the conservative establishment. Underneath they were still the children who had grown up in suburbs in booming, vibrant congregations with giant youth groups. They carried the camp experience, the joy, and the innocence, as well as the self-sacrificing love of their parents with them. They felt guilty about their choice to belong to their peers, rather than to their family. They felt guilty for having to dismiss part of their parents' worldview.

John and Janine are caring people, sensitized by the experiences of their generation, but they are sensitive in another way also. They were raised comfortably, and their comfort has made them less resilient. They lacked the toughness of their parents' generation and the optimistic conviction that all will work out for the best at all times. They had seen the Vietnam War on television through coverage that pulled no punches and covered up no pain or anxiety. Increasing despair and crime in the cities, brought to a climax once again in the Los Angeles riots, accentuated their fear. This side of Janine and John was strengthened as they raised their children in a world they increasingly distrusted.

Thus we see two sides of John and Janine. The experimenting, positive, open- and change-oriented side, and the fearful, suspicious side that encourages them to hide and not risk. They represent two distinct worldviews and two distinct identities. Their sense of belonging in the church mostly confirms the first identity and worldview, while their sense of belonging in their nuclear family tends to confirm the other. Fortunately their faith as Christians tips them over to the positive side.

Their identifications are mixed also. Their identifications with their parents, as well as their identifications with pastors and other young people as they were growing up, were positive. They were profoundly influenced by national leaders such as the Kennedys and Martin Luther King. They did not idolize them, yet these figures had become symbols to them of idealism, empowerment, hope, and compassion.

If caregivers are to be effective, it would be useful if they could write about themselves in the way Janine and John have been described in this chapter. Naturally, the description above is rather simplistic. For instance, John and Janine were described as a couple for the sake of the illustration, while in fact they are two very different people.

First, it is important for caregivers to have a dynamic understanding of their own self-image. What do they see as their strengths in ministry? To what extent is the identity of their childhood still part of their current self-image? In what ways are their identities in process?

Second, caregivers need to know where they feel they belong. Which groups of people would they most gladly spend time with? Which groups make them feel most comfortable? Why is that? Is it because the people in those groups enhance their self-image, or because they truly feel a part of that group, accepted as they really are? Are they perhaps in process from belonging to one group to belonging to another. Do they have a grief reaction to that experience?

Third, caregivers need to be clear about their worldview. People frequently are not totally straightforward about their worldview because they are afraid it will affect their sense of belonging. What is the pastor's worldview about a variety of issues such as sex, homosexuality, marriage, biblical interpretation, lifestyle, child rearing, and so forth? Everyone has certain limits when it comes to accepting the worldviews of others. In general these are issues that go back to questions of love and justice, principles that are understood in most cultures. But there may come a time—if the cross-cultural friction is just too much—when caregivers need to be straightforward about their worldviews but caregivers should not offer their own worldviews before care seekers have had a chance to present their whole story.

If caregivers are aware of how they see the world or where they are in process between ways of viewing the world, they are more likely to control their emotional reactions, which might drift to the surface quite unexpectedly.

Fourth, caregivers need to be aware of the identifications that have been crucial in their development and that still have an impact on them. Who were and are the persons they would like to emulate and for what reason? Whose example have they followed in their career? Who are they still trying to please, even though these people may no longer be alive? In addition, which biblical characters have spoken most to them over the years?

Finally, caregivers should realize where the tensions lie within themselves. Is worldview in harmony with identity? How does identity relate to sense of belonging? What about worldview and sense of belonging? What role do identifications play?

I believe this exercise will help pastors discern the dynamics in the life of suffering people who come to them from and with worlds of experience so different from their own and will nudge them toward the identification that enables them to cross cultural boundaries.

A final principle is yielded by this chapter: Caregivers need to be aware of the contents of the diagnostic categories, as well as the lack of integration between these categories, in their own lives, in order to be an integrating influence in the lives of the people they seek to help.

BIBLIOGRAPHY

Books especially useful for further study are annotated.

Acosta, S., et al.
1990 "Counseling Hispanics in the United States."
       The Journal of Pastoral Care. 44: 33–41.
Atkinson, D.R., G. Morten, and D.W. Sue
1989 *Counseling American Minorities: A Cross-Cultural
       Perspective.* 3rd ed. Dubuque: W.C. Brown.
Augsburger, D.
1986 *Pastoral Counseling across Cultures.* Philadelphia: West-
       minster.
       Most useful in providing well researched discussions
       of worldview and offering ethical guidelines for cross-
       cultural pastoral counseling.
1992 *Conflict Mediation across Cultures.* Louisville: West-
       minster John Knox Press.
Axelson, J.A.
1985 *Counseling and Development in a Multicultural Society.*
       Monterey: Brooks-Cole.
Beek, A.M. van
1987 "Pastoral Counseling Challenges in the Javanese Hos-
       pital." *Pastoral Psychology.* 36: 112–22.
Benedict, R.
1989 *Patterns of Culture.* Boston: Houghton Mifflin.

Brislin, R.
    1981   *Cross-Cultural Encounters.* New York: Pergamom.
    1986   *Intercultural Interactions.* Beverly Hills: Sage.
Clements, W.M., and H.W. Stone, editors
    1991   *Handbook for Basic Types of Pastoral Care and Counseling.* Nashville: Abingdon.
            Relevant articles by Masamba ma Mpolo and Paul Schurman.
Dillard, J.M.
    1983   *Multicultural Counseling.* Chicago: Nelson Hall.
            Especially useful in the area of cross-cultural skills.
Douglas, M.
    1973   *Natural Symbols: Explorations in Cosmology.* Harmondsworth: Penguin.
Gaw, A., editor
    1982   *Cross-Cultural Psychiatry.* Boston: John Wright.
            Covers generic issues and needs of specific cultural groups in North America.
Geertz, C.
    1973   *The Interpretation of Cultures.* New York: Basic.
            Important essays from a symbolic anthropologist's perspective.
Hefner, P., and W.D. Schroeder, editors
    1976   *Belonging and Alienation.* Chicago: Center for the Scientific Study of Religion.
            Explores belonging, especially with regard to religious worldview.
Hsu, Francis
    1971   "Psychological Homeostasis and Jen." *American Anthropologist.* 73: 23–44.
Kakar, S., editor
    1979   *Identity and Adulthood.* Delhi: Oxford University Press.
            Evaluates Erikson's identity theory in the light of Indian culture.
Kaplan, M.
    1976   *Alienation and Identification.* New York: Free Press.

Leach, E.
1976   *Culture and Communication.* Cambridge: Cambridge University Press.
        Provides an interesting analytical view of communication and culture.

Lee, D.
1957   *Freedom and Culture.* Englewood Cliffs: Prentice Hall.

Marsella, A.
1979   *Perspectives on Cross-Cultural Psychology.* New York: Academic Press.

Marsella, A., R. Tharp, and T. Ciborowski, editors
1981   *Cross-Cultural Counseling and Psychotherapy.* New York: Pergamom.

Pedersen, P., et al., editors
1981   *Counseling across Cultures,* rev. and exp. Honolulu: University of Hawaii. Hawaii Press.
        Covers generic issues and discusses approaches with specific cultural groups.

Rotter, J.
1966   "Generalized Expectancies for Internal versus External Control of Reinforcement." *Psychological Monographs.* 80: 1–28.

Samovar, L., and R. Porter, editors
1976   *Intercultural Communication.* Belmont: Wadsworth.

Shweder, R., and R.A. LeVine, editors
1984   *Culture Theory.* Cambridge: Cambridge University Press.
        Very informative essays on the subject of person, culture and emotion.

Sue, D. W., and D. Sue
1990   *Counseling the Culturally Different,* 2nd ed. New York: John Wiley.
        The most comprehensive book on the issues of cross-cultural counseling. It can already be considered a classic text. Replaces the 1981 edition by D.W. Sue (with contributing authors) but does not quite supersede it.

Silva-Netto, B.
  1992   "Pastoral Counseling in a Multicultural Context." *Journal of Pastoral Care*. 46: 131–40.
Strong, S.R.
  1969   "Counseling: An Interpersonal Influence Process." *Journal of Counseling Psychology*. 15: 215–24.
Wicks, R.J., and B.K. Estadt, editors
  1993   *Pastoral Counseling in a Global Church*. Maryknoll, N.Y.: Orbis.
          Caregivers share their experiences in counseling in different countries around the world.
Wimberly, E.P.
  1991   *African-American Pastoral Care*. Nashville: Abingdon.
          Advocates the creative use of story in pastoral care.